MW01264682

# MORE PRAISE FOR SELL EASY!

*At last, a book that fills the gaps in all the other courses and books in sales and marketing. Love those examples, examples, examples!*
Dianna Booher, President, Booher Consultants
and Author of 36 books including *Communicate with Confidence* and
*Winning Sales Letters*

*I'm convinced: there is no magic in sales — but if there were, it would be in this Thom Winninger volume. Winninger is a master in turning the sale in your favor. And you'll get this world class sales-man as your personal sales consultant to boot!*
Ty Boyd
Chairman, Ty Boyd Executive Learning Systems

*Does this book have creditability? Yes! Will it help me develop my own uniqueness for selling? Yes! Will it help me measurably increase my sales production? Yes! Should I buy this book now? Yes!!!*
Danny Cox, Speaker and Author of
*Leadership When the Heat's On* and *There are No Limits*

*"Sell Easy!" is a clear roadmap for anyone who desires to be a wiser, better prepared and resilient sales professional. Apply these princi-ples in this book and watch your business grow and personal fulfill-ment increase.*
Roger Crawford President, Crawford and Associates
and Author of *How High Can You Bounce?*

*This is a unique book among the thousands of "sales" books. Everyone who is selling (and that's all of us) should read it — twice! Thom has done it again with this book. A winner!*
Bert Decker, Chairman
Decker Communications, Inc.

*It is EASY to see that "Sell Easy!" is one of the most helpful, insightful and powerful books ever written on the art of selling.*
Scott McKain, CSP, CPAE
President, McKain Performance Group

*Finally a hard-hitting, concise practical sales guide from a seasoned professional. A solid blueprint for pricing, marketing and selling without compromise.*
Chuck Reaves, CSP, CPAE
President, 21 Associates
Author of: *Never Take Money From a Stranger*

*In "Sell Easy!" Thom has gifted us with a powerful encyclopedia of strategies for envisioning, creating and actualizing a uniqueness in the marketplace that brings our client to a position of "yes!"*
Naomi Rhode, CSP, CPAE
Vice President, Smart Practice

*Who said you can't teach an old dog new tricks? After a half-century of selling "my way" it would have made my life and my time more productive had I been selling "The Winninger Way."*
J.P. (Joe) Cleary, President
Royal Flush Gaming, Ltd.

# SELL EASY

## What to Do
## and Say to
## Get More Yes

Thomas J. Winninger

ST. THOMAS PRESS
Minneapolis, Minnesota

Copyright © 1999 by Thomas J. Winninger

*All rights reserved.* No part of this book may be reproduced or transmitted in any form or by any means, electronic or mechanical, including photocopying, recording, or by any information storage and retrieval system, without permission in writing from the publisher.

Published by *St. Thomas Press*
3300 Edinborough Way, #701
Minneapolis, MN  55435

Publisher's Cataloging-in-Publication Data
Winninger, Thomas, J.
   Sell easy:what to do and say to get more yes/ Thomas J. Winninger –
Minneapolis, MN: St. Thomas Press, 1999.
      p.   cm.
      Includes bibliographical references and index.
      ISBN 0-9638735-0-4
      ISBN 0-9638735-1-2 (pbk.)
   1. Selling.  I. Title.

| HF5438.25 .W56 | 1999 | 99-90340 |
| --- | --- | --- |
| 658.85 | dc—21 | CIP |

*Editorial development by Mary Jo Buday*

PROJECT COORDINATION BY JENKINS GROUP, INC.

03  02  01  00  ◆  5  4  3  2  1

Printed in the United States of America

*This book is lovingly dedicated to my father,*
*Larry Winninger, a great friend, a wonderful mentor,*
*and a superlative salesperson.*
*The appreciation I have for helping people take*
*advantage of great products and services was*
*nurtured in me from my birth.*
*God bless, you, Dad, for all you are and all you've*
*been to me. Your legacy lives with me forever.*

# CONTENTS

# CONTENTS

## PART III: GETTING THE YES

# ACKNOWLEDGMENTS

WRITING A BOOK IS A LIFELONG EXPERIENCE. PUTTING IT INTO words is nothing more than the culmination of a series of events that happen in one's career. This book emerged from 21 years of experience in selling many different products and services. It came as a revelation to me of what sales really is. It's an opportunity to identify people's needs and wants and match those with your products and services, and then make it easy for them to make the decision related to the best choices for their specific situation.

My wife, Lynne, has been a lifelong partner and has helped me stay committed to this process of personal and business development.

Let me also thank all my customers and clients. All the people over the years who have confided in me their needs and wants, motivations and urgencies. All those who have excitedly taken advantage of the products and services that I have provided them.

I also would like to especially thank Thom Norman, the person who helped me understand the process of sharing concepts with other people. A person who exemplifies what it takes to bring structure and discipline to your life; to stay focused and committed to that one thing that brings you to the passion of your career.

I also thank the many authors, writers, and sales professionals who have helped me hone and nurture the focus of *Sell Easy*:

Brian Tracy, a prolific author and good friend.

Tommy Hopkins, who in the early part of my career shared with me the philosophy of knowing what you need to say and when you need to say it.

Harvey Mackay, who helped me understand the importance of self-promotion and who has been kind enough to endorse my book, *Full Price: How to Ask For and Get What You're Worth*.

Jeff Slutsky, who reminded me that sales is not just selling, but street smart marketing.

Jack Canfield and Mark Victor Hanson, authors of *Chicken Soup for the Soul*, who taught me that everybody inside them has a great story to tell.

Neal Rackham, author of *Spin Selling*, who brought to the table important research around how and why people really buy.

Ken Blanchard, author of *The One Minute Manager* and a person who reminds me, if you can say it in a few words, why are you spending time saying it in thousands of words.

Don Hutson, author of many books, but to me most importantly the book, *The Sale*. Don encouraged me to the platform and challenged me to share my ideas in public forums.

Murray Raphel, author of *Mind Your Own Business*, for his

ACKNOWLEDGMENTS

encouragement to see sales and a sales career as a business, with specific focus and challenges.

Thank you, Michael Gerber, for your wonderful writing, The *E-Myth*, which taught me that success is a process, not just an idea.

Zig Ziglar, one of the first speakers I ever had a chance to hear, who encouraged me and reminded me that something deep within you and something in heaven must be married together to have a successful life.

John Livingston, the great barnstorming pilot who dies long before I was born, who inspired the book, *Jonathon Livingston Seagull* by Richard Bach. Fly high, Jonathon; stretch yourself, Jonathon; take risks, Jonathon; it builds character.

Bob Tucker for his wonderful book, *Managing the Future*, who reminded me that selling is not a static environment but something that must be married to the trends affecting our customers and clients.

And finally, Nido Qubein, a friend and confidante and certainly one of the greatest thinkers of our time, author of many books, confidante to global leaders, and entrepreneur extraordinaire.

# INTRODUCTION

THE CHALLENGE FOR YOU TODAY IS HOW TO IMPROVE YOUR sales, in a limited amount of time, at a level that grows your business. There's a significant difference between having knowledge and being able to implement that knowledge at a level that has some net effect. To be able to do today versus to know things is critical.

Can you use your knowledge to help your customers buy? Can you use the tools you've learned to help your product get to the market more effectively? Can you use your training to make your job easier and to improve your productivity by solving some of the challenges that you face over and over and over again? If you cannot do these things with your knowledge, then what is its value?

*Sell Easy: Proven Techniques for a Rewarding Career in Sales* focuses on skills that are proven to result in a higher level of success. After you read this book and begin to apply the information to your sales environment, I guarantee you will have a greater awareness of your products, services, and customers — which will help you sell easy and lead to a growth in your net business.

I've been in sales for more than twenty years. During that time I have attended numerous sales training courses, as you probably have. I can tell you some of the things I learned at these seminars, but mostly I can tell you what I didn't learn. I can tell you the things that I was challenged on while working my business, situations that weren't discussed in any of the training courses.

For example, what do you do when a customer says, "I think the price you charge is a little high"? I don't recall one sales seminar that taught me how to respond effectively in that environment. I heard tips on how to deal with a reluctant customer and how to overcome objections — but this critical scenario was not addressed — and we've all been there.

Although I had to learn how to deal with this situation on my own, you're in luck. Bound between these two covers is the experience I've acquired over the years. I will guide you in the preparation of quality responses to "Your price is a little high." I will discuss the essentials for a successful business career: defining your uniqueness in the marketplace, determining a buying model of your best customers, asking the right questions, building functional responses, and selling to your customers' needs.

This book is organized in three parts: preparation, presentation, and getting the yes. Examples of various sales environments are provided throughout the book, so you can see how these techniques can help you sell easy and lead you to greater success. By polishing your skills to a level where you are able to respond in any given situation, at a heightened level of control, you will reach more gratifying and satisfying conclusions with your customers.

These guidelines can be applied to any sales environment, whether you're in traditional or nontraditional sales, a member of a support team, or selling a product or service.

I challenge you to apply the concepts within this book; to grow your business; to become a stronger, more effective, and happier salesperson — to *Sell Easy* — and to get more yes.

# PART I

## PREPARING FOR THE SALE

# Chapter One

# INCREASE YOUR SALES PROBABILITY

THE GOAL OF MOST SALESPEOPLE IS TO INCREASE THEIR SHARE OF the market. I'd guess that is one of the main reasons you're reading this book: to learn new tips on how to expand your market share and to learn what you can to improve your sales probability. The challenge, of course, is to learn how to be more effective at your job when, for the most part, customers are reluctant to commit to making a purchase. Today, it seems, salespeople hear more objections from their customers than ever before, and the buying cycle seems to get longer and longer. It's no wonder that sales volumes remain stagnant (at best) or decrease (at worst).

Throughout this book I will take you in directions that

have proved to be valuable to me, in terms of gaining customer loyalty and increasing my market share and sales probability.

I like to think of the entire sales presentation as a form of closing. Let me explain. Closing is the point in your demonstration when you want your customer to agree with you — to say, "Yes, I will buy your product." My philosophy is that instead of waiting until the *end* of your presentation to ask for an agreement, you should structure your sales presentation so that you receive several agreements from your customer *throughout* your presentation!

Format your sales presentation so that your customer becomes comfortable saying yes. Then, when you ask for their final commitment, at the end of your presentation, it isn't a challenge for them. They feel less risk (and fear) about committing and saying yes. This is how you can sell easy and increase your sales probability.

Many salespeople have the talent to make polished presentations. However, if the presentation isn't focused on the customer's needs there is a greater chance that the sale will be lost.

To discover information about your customers, it is essential for you to ask them questions early in your business relationship. Without this vital data even the smoothest sales presentation can be ineffective if it is not tailored to that particular customer's greatest need.

Consider this: how do you respond to cold calls from telemarketers? Are you receptive to their sales message? No. The telemarketer doesn't know your needs — and therefore is unable to spark your interest.

By preparing a thorough sales presentation based on information you have received from your customer, you can sell easy and increase your probability of success. Some important questions to ask your customers:

1. What are their needs and wants? (Chapter 9)

2. What is their financial capability? What are their budget restrictions? (Chapter 15)

3. How close is your product or service to what they need? (Chapter 2)

4. What is their specific time frame? Do they intend on making a purchase — or are they simply shopping around? (Chapter 15)

5. Who has the authority to make the final decision?

6. Is there any reason for your customer not to do business with you? How open are they to your product and service? Perhaps they've had difficulty with your company in the past, or their computer system isn't compatible with the products you sell, or you can't meet a certain specification, etc. You don't want to discover at the end of your sales presentation that there is an impediment to your customer purchasing from you. (Chapter 14)

The answers to these questions should significantly affect the direction and content of your sales presentation.

Remember your goal is to get confirmations along the way instead of waiting until the end. Confirmations are: "Yes. I have the authority to make the purchase." or "Yes. This is the level we have budgeted." or "Yes. If you show me something I like, I'm willing to purchase from you." These pre-agreements will increase the probability that you close the sale.

Three sell easy approaches to increase your sales probability:

**Approach Number One:** Close to your customer's needs and wants. Instead of discussing a lot of features and details about your product, focus your demonstration on how your product or service satisfies each customer's specific needs.

**Approach Number Two:** Close to the conditions that will satisfy your customer. What conditions of satisfaction do they have? Determine any conditions up front and then explain how your product satisfies the conditions.

The following types of questions can help you discover the conditions your customer may have:

♦   What product do you want? Are there size limitations?

♦   What do you expect after the purchase? Are there any production goals that must be met?

♦   What factors will determine your final decision? Is a certain quantity needed by a specific date?

The more you know about your customer, the more likely you are to increase your success in sales.

**Approach Number Three:** Close to the decision-making process. Find out who has the authority to make the final decision. Are there any budget restrictions?

## SELL EASY RULES

**Rule Number One: Establish conditions of satisfaction.** Ask your customer for two or three conditions that are essential for them to commit to a purchase.

**Rule Number Two: Seek serious, continual confirmations.** Pose questions that will generate pre-agreements or confirmations throughout your presentation. Pre-agreements tend to heighten your customer's commitment level before you reach the point of asking them for a final yes.

**Rule Number Three: Clarify their decision-making process.** Avoid waiting until the end of your sales demonstration to discover details about your customer's decision-making authority. Some salespeople telephone their customers in advance of meeting with them for the sole purpose of inquiring about the decision-making process of their customer's company. This way the salesperson is informed about what type of buying cycle to expect.

**Rule Number Four:** Learn how to overcome resistance. Resistance is a natural element in all sales and business transactions. A successful salesperson knows how to handle resistance in a positive way. (Chapter 14)

## REVIEW

The more effort you put into getting to know your customer and preparing your sales presentation — the more your sales probability will increase. The key is to ask questions so that you know who your customer is and are able to tailor your products' features to their needs. The following sell easy chapters take you through the necessary steps get more yes.

## SELL EASY TIPS

♦   Structure sales presentation so that you receive several agreements from your customer throughout the demonstration — not just at the end.

♦ From beginning to end — your sales presentation should be looked upon as a form of closing.

♦ A polished sales presentation is ineffective if it is not focused on each customer's greatest need.

8

# Chapter Two

# DEFINE YOUR CATEGORY AUTHORITY

MORE CONSUMERS THAN EVER BEFORE ARE SAVVY SHOPPERS — and fast talk and a smooth presentation won't guarantee a yes. Even if you are a skilled communicator, your success in sales will be fleeting if you don't know what sets your product or service apart from your competitors'.

The marketplace is cluttered with businesses that provide similar services and products. In order to succeed, you must distinguish yourself and your product or service. How can you do this?

Before you solicit sales, either in the field, over the telephone or via the Internet, you need to answer three basic questions:

- ♦ What am I selling?
- ♦ How is my product unique from my competitors'?
- ♦ Who is my customer?

If you are able to answer these questions, you will have a stronger foothold in your market. The better able you are to state your *category authority*, your uniqueness, the more appealing you will be to your customers and the easier it will be for you to acquire sales and to grow your business. Ultimately, your customers will feel confident in working with you because they will know what and why they are buying from you.

Your category authority is what distinguishes you from your competition in the marketplace. Once you determine and then explain your uniqueness, your competitive position will be secure. Your customers will understand why they should do business with you — and not someone else. The stronger you have defined your category authority in the minds and hearts of your customers the more likely they are to be devoted to you, and the more your market dominance is assured, both for yourself as a salesperson and for your company.

Sell Easy Examples:

In the past Carrier concentrated on selling furnaces. Today, they sell "comfort systems." A couple of years ago their market researchers determined that a home-owner would purchase comfort more readily than a furnace. People don't want to know they own a furnace, per se, because if they are aware that they own a furnace, chances are something is wrong with it and it needs repair. It is not providing them comfort. Thus, Carrier stated that its category authority is providing comfort systems.

The result: homeowners go to Carrier seeking comfort — not just a furnace. And they typically will pay more for the comfort, without minding the extra cost.

Kodak sells "capturing life's magic moments forever" — not film. When someone buys Kodak film they pay extra for the guarantee of having magic moments last forever. Kodak's category authority is capturing life's magic moments — for a slightly higher price than other film companies.

## WHAT IS YOUR CATEGORY AUTHORITY?

To define your category authority, there are four questions to answer about the product or service you sell:

1.  Who are you?

    In other words, what are you or your company number one at? For example, Wal-Mart advertises, "We sell for less." That is their category authority. What is yours? The argument that "everyone can't be number one" is not a valid reason for failing to state your category authority. There are enough categories available for you to pick one thing that you're better at than anyone else is. Take the time to determine what it is because your category authority will set you apart from others in your market. Why should a customer purchase your product or service versus the "other company"?

*Customers pay for your uniqueness.*

2. What are you doing?

   In twenty-four words or less explain, from a customer standpoint, what you do. What benefits do you ensure your customers? Carrier, for example, utilizes technology to ensure a determined comfort level in any room or zone of a home. If a customer wants one area warmer or cooler than another, Carrier ensures that the customer gets it.

   Sell Easy Example:

   A small business owner sells lawn mowers. Is he going to sell mowers or is he going to help customers obtain beautiful yards? If he sells beautiful yards he is going to be more successful than if he only sells mowers. Why? Because there are thousands of people who sell lawn mowers — but few sell beautiful yards. By focusing on beautiful yards he can sell a greater variety of products to meet all of his customers' lawn care needs.

3. Who are you doing it for?

   Who is your customer? (See Chapter 2) Do you have more than one type of customer? You must identify all of them. What are their needs? The umbrella question is "What does your primary customer buy from you?" not "What do you sell?"

The difference between defining what you do and what your customer buys is a critical component in business today. Your uniqueness is what your customer pays for.

*You must be able to quantifiably benchmark your differences.*

4. What makes you different?

You need to determine five things that make you or your company different. By doing this you will be prepared to provide a quality response in any given sales environment by accentuating your uniqueness. In any situation, with any customer, it is your response that will count. Research shows that more customers seek a quality response from a salesperson rather than low price. What's your quality response going to be?

Sell Easy Example:

Tires Galore charges $600 for a set of radial tires. Wheels R Us charges $500 for a set of radial tires. If Tires Galore defines the uniqueness of their radial tires, then in reality they are only charging $100 for their product. If they can define the uniqueness of their set of tires (free tire rotation every 5,000 miles and free repair for the life of the tires), to offset the price difference, it's much easier for the customer to say, "Gee. It would be ridiculous for me not to spend $100 for all of this. Look at the extra benefits I get for only $100."

But, if Tires Galore only discusses the similarities between their radial tires and Wheels R Us' tires, they have failed to quantifiably benchmark their uniqueness. Customers will take their business to Wheels R Us rather than spend $100 extra for the same product.

Let me repeat: you must quantifiably benchmark your differences. You can't just say, "We do a better job." Or "We'll service you more effectively." Or "Our equipment is of a higher quality." Or "We're faster." None of these are quantifiable statements. Instead of "We're faster" you could say, "We have a twenty-four hour toll-free customer service hotline that is answered within three rings by a person who knows how to get you the help you need to solve your problem." That's quantifiable.

Or you could say, "To ensure that you're never without a laptop, whenever your laptop needs servicing, we will lend you a similar laptop to use while we repair yours." That's definable. That's your uniqueness.

## SELL EASY RULES

**Rule Number One: Your value is your uniqueness.** If you know things that your customers need to know and they don't know where to find the information, the knowledge you have is your uniqueness. It makes you valuable to them.

As a customer, I want to be called on by sales professionals who know things I should know, especially when I don't know where to find the information. In contrast, I don't want to be called on by salespeople who know a lot about their product. I can easily find well-trained salespeople. Product training is rampant. For instance, if a computer salesperson comes into my business and he only talks about his computer -not about my business — he is not unique. He is not valuable to me.

**Rule Number Two: Uniqueness is more than a product or service.** Your product or service doesn't have to be original. Your uniqueness could be something as simple as knowing how your product or service applies to a specific business or industry. You can establish your value by identifying a unique element of your product or service to your customer.

Sell Easy Example:

I need a computer for my office. I am much more interested in knowing what a computer can do for me than the actual hardware. So I go to a computer store, one with a big storefront and computers throughout the floor. I walk in and say, "I want to buy a computer." If the salesperson asks the right questions he will learn I want to manage my client list to the point where I can categorize my clients and reach them more effectively through the use of a database management system. If, however, the salesperson immediately starts talking about RAM and megabytes and printers, rather than asking me questions, what happens? My resistance level goes up because I don't understand how these elements will help me achieve my goal. I don't want to understand the equipment. I want to understand how to make it do what I want it to do as fast as I want it done. If the salesperson can define what a particular computer can do for me, he will be met with less resistance. And, I'll even be willing to spend more money for his computer — because I will pay more to get exactly what I want.

**Rule Number Three: State your category authority.** Define a position that only you have in a category — a category in which you can take the number one position. By determining your customer's needs (see Chapter 9) you'll be better able to determine your category authority.

A computer manufacturer might say, "We make a computer that is expressly designed for people who work out of their homes." That is a their category.

> ***Caution:*** *Don't define a category that is too narrow, as it could negatively impact the size of your market.*

**Rule Number Four: Build your position up rather than tearing down someone else's.** You are not going to obtain a number one position in a category by identifying another competitor and saying, "This is how we differ from them." When you do this, what you're saying is, "Hey, there's someone else in the marketplace like me." Chances are your customer will then look for them.

After you establish your category authority do not compare yourself to a competitor. The sell easy choice is to create an advisory board of your best customers (see Chapter 3) and benchmark your uniqueness to your customers' needs, not away from your competition. By setting up an advisory board of your best customers, you can remain in the number one position in your category authority, even as your best customers' needs change.

> Sell Easy Examples:
>
> Years ago the joke was that people who managed the train industry considered themselves to be in the train business instead of seeing themselves in the transportation business. The result of this narrow thinking is that today the train industry is not very competitive.
>
> As a comparison, look at the airline industry. The majority of airlines aren't only concerned with filling their seats with people, they want to fill the cargo of their jets with merchandise. Instead of focusing on only filling their passenger seats, they realized the economic benefit of transporting cargo. As a result, the airline industry is still a viable means of transportation.

Consider the neighborhood hardware store. Even with

the proliferation of large warehouse stores, these small hardware stores are gaining momentum in the marketplace because they are positioning themselves as the do-it-yourself center. "Make weekend projects fun," they advertise. As a homeowner I am apt to attend a free "Plumbing Made Easy" presentation on a Saturday morning. And chances are I'll walk out of the store with the tools necessary for any plumbing problem that might befall my household.

## REVIEW

Your challenge is to more effectively define your uniqueness with your customers. This vital information will set you apart from the competition — and help you produce more sales.

After you've identified your category authority you'll need to determine who is the most likely benefactor of your uniqueness. You can do this by establishing a buying model of your best customers.

## SELL EASY TIPS

♦ Define your category authority to distinguish yourself from the competition.

♦ Customers are willing to pay for uniqueness.

♦ Instead of tearing down the competition, quantifiably benchmark your differences.

♦ Answer the four questions about product uniqueness in relationship to what you sell.

♦ Learn to effectively present the uniqueness of your product and service to your customers.

Chapter Three

# DEVELOP A BUYING MODEL

HAVE YOU EVER QUESTIONED THE LOGIC OF TRAINING PEOPLE IN sales techniques, sending them out into the market with various products or services — and then *hoping* that the training pays off and they close some sales? Sadly, many organizations train their sales staffs in this manner, with minimal results.

My philosophy is that rather than focusing on *selling*, you should learn how to *help a customer buy from you*. If you can educate potential customers about the value they will receive from purchasing your product or service, you will have a stronger success rate than someone who knows sales techniques but can't explain to a potential customer (or an established customer) why the customer should buy from them.

The first step in learning how to help a customer buy from you is to determine the makeup of your customer base. Even if you think the majority of your customers know why they should buy from you, the reality is they probably do not. Basically there are three types of customers:

♦ Premium Customers

♦ Low-Price Customers

♦ Uninformed Customers

About seventeen percent of your customers are **premium** customers. These customers are loyal to you and/or your company. After numerous business transactions, you have an established and well-nurtured relationship with them. They trust you.

These premium buyers know the value of your product and service. They are not interested in shopping around for the lowest price or a different model because they are confident in you. They would buy other products that you sell. They desire a long-term relationship based on trust, not low price.

About twenty-seven percent of your customers do not seek a relationship. They want the **lowest price**. They base their purchase decisions on cost only. They're not looking for frills or add-on value after the transaction is completed. Their only concern is to spend as little money up front as possible. (Exception: as customers age, they tend to become concerned about a product's durability. They want products that will last longer.)

What about the remaining fifty-six percent of your customer base? Amazingly enough, this majority consists of the *uninformed* customer. They do not know how to buy. They don't know what to expect or what to ask for — because they have not been taught. They aren't sure if price or quality (value) should be their primary concern. And the more they shop around, the more confused they become. They are unable to easily sort through the proliferation of advertising that they see and hear.

To expand your market and to increase your sales you must know how to reach the uninformed majority. If you can educate this group about why they need your product or service, and how they would benefit from your product or service, your business will grow.

How can you reach the uninformed majority? What will you tell them? To answer these questions you must turn to your premium customers, your best buyers, and *develop a buying model*. This buying model will be based on the benefits of the products and services that attract and keep your best customers loyal to you.

Your buying model will give you the key to acquire and maintain new customers. It will be your advantage over other sales people. As we've already established, there is an abundance of sales training courses available. What you will have that others won't is the skill to help a customer buy.

When you reach the fifty-six percent group of uninformed customers and let them know why your primary customers buy from you, you will have set yourself apart from the competition. Remember that your category authority is the key to your success. When you explain your uniqueness you will distinguish yourself in your customer's mind — and you will be more likely to acquire their business.

Additionally, by sharing your uniqueness with these uninformed customers you are giving them knowledge that will stimulate their interest in you. They will begin to ask questions. It is beneficial to you when customers question and seek information from the competition. The more questions they ask of you and others, the more evident your uniqueness will become. You will distance yourself from any competition a potential customer may have thought you had.

> Sell Easy Example:
>
> When you ask a customer, "What are you doing to create viability for your product by value-adding your product in a competitive market?" you are giving them a question you want them to ask you.

To create your buying model, answer the following six questions about your primary customers. These questions can be applied to any sales environment, regardless if you are selling a product or a service.

## BUYING MODEL QUESTIONS

1.  Who are your best customers?
    The first step is to identify your best customers. Be aware that your premium customers aren't necessarily the ones who spend the most money with you. Sometimes a customer who purchases the greatest amount is beating you up on price. That's right. He may belong to the twenty-seven percent who purchase based on price alone. He might buy so much of your product that he has actually leveraged you against price. He assumes you fear losing his business because of the volumes he purchases. There is

no loyalty in this relationship, even though the volume may be significant.

Do you have a customer who requires a lot of service? Do some customers place minimal demands on you or your company? Oftentimes customers who demand a lot of service tend to be less valuable. Why? Because you do not charge them for the service you provide. Therefore your margin goes down the more time you spend on their account. Reconsider labeling someone a "best customer" if you have to call on him three times a day to keep him happy.

Sell Easy Example:

Some fast food restaurants tried to model their structure based on input from customers who frequented different fast food restaurants. The result was that a lot of mistakes were made before they identified who their customers were and what they wanted.

With a best customer it could be frequency, number of products and services they buy from you, what they buy from you, or their value in terms of margin.

**Caution:** *Don't go to one of your competitors to find out who their best customers are. More than likely their customers buy from them for different reasons than your best customers buy from you. You must use your customers to develop your buying model.*

2.  What are your best customers' highest needs? Some companies actually brand their best customers by labeling a product "Platinum" or "Gold." A company might market a new product or service

to their "performance" customers or "express" customers exclusively. Of course, the purpose of the new program is to satisfy their best customers' needs. The logic is simple: similar customers may have similar needs. If you design a program based on your best customers' needs — and you market that program to people who are uninformed — you can generate more best customers. Remember: uninformed customers may simply not know they have the need — until you educate them!

3.   What is the most important value you bring to your best customers?

Irrespective of their highest need, in twenty-four words or less define what you bring to your best customers. What value do your products or services provide? How do your best customers benefit most from what you sell them?

Sell Easy Example:

The greatest value Hertz brings to its customers is getting them out of the airport and moving toward their final destinations faster than any other rental car agency.

When selecting the most important value you provide, consider that a service-based value usually lasts longer than a product value. Hertz, for example, advertises that they are superior in getting customers to their destinations with the most ease and in the least amount of time. They are promoting their service as opposed to trying to establish the quality of their fleet of cars as being superior to those of other rental car agencies.

If you sell a function of service, it's easier to maintain the number one position. Products, on the other hand, typically have life cycles. That is why technology-driven companies, like Intel and Microsoft, spend billions of dollars continually trying to improve the technology of their products. Their sales are driven by the ingenuity of their products — not on the services they provide.

4.  What do your best customers buy from you?

    Are their similarities among your best customers? What is the primary cluster of products or services that your best customers buy? Once you've taken the time to analyze what products and services your best customers buy from you — you may be surprised. You may learn that what you think is the most valuable service or product you offer is not what actually attracts your best customers!

5.  How do your best customers buy from you?

    Do your best customers make their purchases over the telephone or do they demand to see you in person when making a purchase? Are most of your sales generated via the Internet — or by referral? Once you determine how your best customers typically buy from you, build that particular value into your buying model.

    For instance, if they need to see you, then set-up a way for your customers (existing and potential) to see you.

    Sell Easy Example:

    When you meet with a new customer, explain that the reason you're meeting with them personally is because your best customers demand — and receive — this kind of personalized service. By this comment, you are teaching this new customer that if a competitor is trying to sell to them over the phone, instead of in person, they aren't receiving "best customer" treatment.

6.   How frequently do your best customers buy?

One of the biggest mistakes salespeople make is to assume that the frequency of contact should be equal to the frequency of purchase. Many of your best customers might not buy *frequently*, and therefore, you probably don't service them frequently. If this is true, you could be at risk of losing some of your best customers.

If a best customer buys monthly, you should contact them in between their purchases. Fax them information. Mail them a note. Don't rely on the monthly one-on-one meetings to keep their loyalty. Don't forfeit contact with a primary customer to spend time with a demanding customer who is buying less and whose loyalty is uncertain. If you fail to contact your premium customer because you're too busy meeting the demands of the low-price customer you risk losing the better account. Eventually you could regret spending the time you did on the low-price customer.

Sell Easy Example:

A colleague of mine has great customers who call on him once a month to place an order. My colleague calls on his other (unreliable) customers three times a month — because they demand the attention. Realize these demanding customers aren't nearly as loyal as his primary customers, yet they get more of his time and attention. What happens? By neglecting his primary customers, he risks losing their business.

If you devote the time to develop a buying model, and use it, your market share will increase because of your improved ability to help customers buy from you. The information you compile on your best customers will enable you to attract new customers who are in the fifty-six percent group.

After these potential customers listen to your information, they will begin to ask questions. The answers they receive from you and your competition will help them realize and appreciate your uniqueness. Additionally, they will be more willing to pay for your uniqueness and your selling power will increase through buyer modeling.

## SELL EASY RULES

**Rule Number One: Define the characteristics of your best buyer.** How often do your best customers buy? How much attention do they need? What services appeal to them?

Sell Easy Example:

When I purchased my car, as a premium customer I received a special service contract. Every time I put 2,800 miles on my car, the car dealership will pick up my car from my house, drive it to their service center, service it through the night, and return it to my house before I need it the next morning. That is premium service, and I love it. Although the dealer does not charge me for the pick up and delivery of my car, I'm certain they charge me a premium price for the work they perform once my car is in the shop. Do I argue with their fees? Absolutely not. The convenience of having my car serviced while I'm sleeping, without the hassle of dropping it off and picking it up myself, is a premium need that I have — and I am willing to pay for it.

**Rule Number Two: Educate your buyers.** Education is achieved by asking questions. If you provide your customers with questions they should be asking you, they will begin to question your competition as well. The responses they receive from your competition will benefit you.

Sell Easy Example:

Financial institutions that advertise "buy a certificate of deposit from us because we have the lowest rate" are only stimulating questions based on price. If, however, they advertised, "Most of our customers have been with us for years. Our customers stay with us because, in addition to offering competitive rates on our certificates of deposit and other savings programs, we help manage their security for a better retirement" they would encourage consumers to question the services provided by other financial institutions.

Some salespeople ask their customers, "Do you have any questions?" Realize this technique will not work with fifty-six percent of your customer base — because they do not have enough information to ask questions. You must give them the questions to ask.

*Provide customers with questions that low-price sellers cannot answer. Your response is more important to a customer, not low price.*

**Rule Number Three: Increase the quantity and quality of your contact with your best customers.** The frequency of purchase should not dictate the frequency of your contact with your customer. The contact you have with them between purchases is your frequency. Are you mailing thank-you notes? Are you faxing agendas of what you will talk about with them the next time you get together in the purchase environment? Keep in contact in between purchases.

Sell Easy Example:

Every 2,800 miles the dealership I purchased my car from increases the frequency of contact with me, a best customer. They wash my car while they have it. They deliver the car to my garage. They put a note on the dashboard stating what they're going to do next time they have my car in the shop. They have a tire on/off program. In the fall they take off the summer tires and put on the winter tires. They store my summer tires. That's all contact. And it is very important, especially in today's competitive market.

**Rule Number Four: Put your best customers on your advisory board.** Pick out several primary customers and put them on an advisory board. In this position they will be available to alert you to changes in their industry and the market. As needs change, their advice and input will help you stay onboard.

Meet with your advisory board on a regular basis, so that you continue to redefine your buying model. As the economy and products change, so will your buying model.

**Rule Number Five: Compile a "Target 25" list.** Choose twenty-five of your customers and devise strategies to educate them on what you do and why they should buy what you sell. Over time you will learn to reach out to potential customers effectively, instead of waiting for them to come to you. Your target 25 list can consist of past customers, inac-

---

## Sell Easy Buying Model Sample

1. Who are your best buyers?
   *Corporate businessmen travelling during the week throughout the U.S.*

2. What are your best customers' highest needs?
   *Fast and hassle-free pick up and drop-off of rental cars.*

3. What is the most important value you bring to your best customers?
   *Speed and hassle-free service.*

4. What does your customer buy from you?
   *Dependable service.*

5. How do your best customers buy from you?
   *Over the phone, through travel agents.*

6. How frequently do your best customers buy?
   *Weekly/regularly.*

---

tive customers, or customers with whom you want to have a stronger relationship.

## REVIEW

After you have taken the time to determine your category authority and to develop a buying model you will be far ahead of other salespeople. You now have the ability to explain your uniqueness and you know what types of services and communications are important to your best customers. This knowledge is the base for a successful career in business.

## SELL EASY TIPS

♦ Instead of focusing on selling your product or service learn how to help a customer buy from you.

♦ Develop a buying model based on your best customers' needs.

♦ Market your product or service based on the buying model of your best customers.

♦ Establish an advisory board of your best customers to keep informed of any changes in the markets and industries in which you sell.

# Chapter Four

# BECOME A SPECIALIST

IT SEEMS AS THOUGH EVERY INDUSTRY HAS ITS SPECIALISTS. THESE specialists seem to gain more business and respect from their customers than "the regular guys." In sales it isn't any different. To distinguish yourself from the bunch you must become a **sales** specialist, a **product** specialist, and you also need to specialize in your **customers** and their **environments.**

Customers want critical data facts. They want to know why your product is good and how it applies to them. What has your product's experience been in the past? What features of your product are important to your best customers? You must become a **product specialist** in order to answer these questions.

Another critical data fact is becoming a **sales specialist.** Unless you are an effective salesperson, all of the product knowledge in the world will not enable you to share this information effectively with your customers. You must know how to efficiently apply your product knowledge to your sales environment. You need to understand how to qualify a customer's need, how to give choices, and how to get pre-agreements.

Additionally, you must know your customer — the decision-maker — so well that you know the person. Form a relationship. Understand your customer's needs. Determine why your customer wants to buy. Understand how they buy. Do they base their purchase decision on product or service? Do they use other vendors? Finding the answers to these questions will help you become a **customer specialist**.

> ***Caution:*** *Success in sales requires a balance of the four specialty areas. Someone who is a sales specialist but lacks product knowledge will have difficulty making a sale, as well as someone who has the product knowledge but has difficulty making an effective presentation.*

The final ingredient is to know how your product is used after the sale. In what type of environment is your product used? You must become an **environment specialist** to fully comprehend the importance of your product to your customer. What are the changing needs of your customer's industry? What are your customer's frustrations?

Sell Easy Example:

A salesman for a steel company that produces rolled and cut steel visited one of his manufacturing cus-

tomers. During their conversation the customer men-
tions his frustration of having to send the steel out to a
service center to have it embossed before they can use
the steel in their manufacturing process. Prior to this
conversation the salesman for the steel company was
not aware of his customer's need — nor his frustration.
The salesman returned to the steel company and discussed his customer's problem and need. Eventually, the
salesman was able to return to his customer and offer to
have the steel company emboss the steel before they
sold it to the manufacturer. By learning about the environment in which his customer was using his product,
the salesman increased his value — and took the pressure off of price.

This is the highest level of specialty you can achieve —
going beyond the transaction, getting beyond the education
process, and into the application of your product.

To determine how specialized you are, see how well you
can answer the following questions about your customers:

1.  What do you know about the company that buys
    your product? How much risk are they capable of
    taking? How long has the firm been in business?

2.  Who makes the purchase decision? What do you
    know about the person who does the purchasing?
    How much information do they share with you? Do
    they know what happens after the product is pur-
    chased — especially in a large environment?
    (Surprisingly, some buyers do not know how the
    product is used.)

3.  What do you know about the buyer's application
    and use of your product?

4.   What do you know about their environment? (For example, in a retail environment, there is a lot of pressure on price and convenience. Customers want to buy more things from fewer retailers. This is called single source supply.)

*A specialist at the highest level of the relationship knows what their customer needs to know — and makes themself the primary source of this information.*

Whenever you share information with your customer — especially information that they have a need for — you create a dependency.

My entire business career has been based on the fact that I research my customer's industry so that I learn things that my customer may not yet know. I become aware of probable changes within their industry. Oftentimes my customer doesn't know where to find the answers to meet upcoming changes — so he comes to me in search of information. I have acquired the reputation of being a specialist — and thereby created a dependency on the part of my customer.

## Sᴇʟʟ Eᴀsʏ Rᴜʟᴇs

**Rule Number One: Establish *you* as a value**. The knowledge you bring to your customer, a superior level of facts and information about your customer's environment, makes you valuable. With this extra knowledge *you* meet or exceed the worth of your product.

In other words, if you don't bring something to the business relationship (knowledge) to make you more valuable than the worth of your product, it will be easy for your customer to shop somewhere else for the same value. It will have then come down to a choice between product and product. If, however, you sell knowledge along with your product, you separate yourself from the competition by.

> Sell Easy Example:
>
> You walk into a computer store in search of a new computer and software for your marketing business. If the salesperson begins to talk about RAM and processing speed, rather than how a computer system can better manage your database, you know he or she is not a specialist. You could walk into virtually any computer store and receive the same information. If, however, a salesperson is able to relate their product to your needs, they will most likely get your business because they have expressed a knowledge and understanding of your working environment. Their expertise brings value to the sales transaction — much more so than RAM or processing speed.

**Rule Number Two: Become a full-time student of your customer's environment.** Research and study your customer's industry. Understand the history and projected future developments. Read trade publications. Talk to people in planning about where the see they industry heading.

If you sell to consumers, do you know about their changing needs and habits?

> Sell Easy Example:
>
> If grocers had identified the eat-at-home trend that's popular now, they would have changed the meal replacement strategy before some of the newer restaurants entered the market with meals to go.

Unfortunately, for the most part, grocers did not focus on this changing need of the consumer — to have a meal cooked and ready to serve at home — and they've lost that part of the market.

**Rule Number Three: Learn about the dynamics that relate to your product or service *after* the transaction.** Talk with your customers and question them about what they do with your product. How is it used? The information you receive from them can be valuable in giving you a clear understanding of their environment and how your product or service plays a role in it.

**Rule Number Four: Understand the changing dynamics in sales.** If you are aware of the trends that can affect your market, you can be more effective at selling your product or service. Be aware of the changes that affect your customers and their environments. Some trends today are:

♦ Customers prefer to buy more items from fewer vendors.

♦ Customers delay making a final purchase decision until they've tested the product.

♦ Cost-value perceptions are important. Your value must exceed your price, and you always must be able to explain your differences — your uniqueness — with hard differentiators. Just saying that you're different or better isn't enough. You must explain the difference for your customers, in terms they can relate to.

♦ The decision making process is changing, especially in large sale environments. It is now more common for two or three people to be involved in making a final decision — or a committee — rather than one person.

♦ Changes in technology occur frequently — and quickly. It is amazing the dramatic changes that can occur in technology within only a six or eight-month period. One result of this is that speed is an ever-changing need in many industries. Businesses want things faster and faster. Time is an important commodity.

♦ Usage applications change. For example, at one time monitoring a product's use and solving minor problems required an onsite visit by a technician or other support staff. No longer is that necessary today. With the advances in technology, it is possible to monitor a customer's usage from a distance, as well as assist them with problem solving via the telephone.

♦ Personal dynamism. You must always support the human side of customer relations. Some of the advances in technology make it is easy to stray from the human side of sales. You must be careful of this.

## REVIEW

First and foremost, ask your customers powerful questions about planning and product usage. What are you planning on doing with this product? What environment do you use it in? How do you use the product? What alterations, if any, must you make to the product before using it? What changes do you see in your environment?

The more you understand about the application of your product, whether your product is an educational course, a home appliance or technical service — the more effective you will be in marrying your sales delivery to your customer's need for reliable information. And in your customer's eyes you will be a specialist. They will come to rely on you for more than product.

Secondly, you need to anchor in your best buyers. If you're going to quantify critical data facts around anyone, you want to make sure you're doing it with your best customers (see Chapter 3), then you won't have to worry about the others.

And finally, assume awareness when sharing a trend with a customer.

> Sell Easy Example:
>
> "Mike, I'm sure you know that many people today are outsourcing their steel to have it embossed" is a more effective approach than saying, "Hey, Mike, did you know....?" You want to compliment your buyer on the fact that they probably already know about the changing trends in their industry. Give your customer the benefit of the doubt. Do not make your customer feel stupid because you're a specialist.

## SELL EASY TIPS

- ♦ Learn how your customers utilize your product or service.

- ♦ Make yourself more valuable than the worth of your product — by specializing in your customers' industries.

- ♦ Establish yourself as a specialist by researching the trends in your customers' industries.

Chapter Five

# TAKE CONTROL OF THE BUYING CYCLE

MANY SALESPEOPLE ARE FRUSTRATED BY THE LACK OF LOYALTY THEY receive from their customers. It doesn't seem to matter how good your product is — or what type of service you give them — the probability that your customers will remain loyal to you for their business is slim. The fact is, most customers are not committed enough to return to you for a second or third purchase.

Anyone who has worked in sales realizes that repeat business and referrals are essential to growing a business. Is there a way to work around this lack of commitment? Is there a way to take control?

In a simple word, yes. There are ways in which you can

take control of your customer's buying cycle, and thereby greatly increase your chances of getting their repeat business.

The first step is for you to determine if you're in a large sale environment or a small sale environment. The dynamics involved in selling in these two environments are different, thus the need to differentiate between the two. One of the most important differences is the number of contacts you will have with your customer during a sales transaction. (I will discuss this in greater detail later in this chapter.)

## THE BUYING CYCLE

Before you can take control of the buying cycle, it is necessary for you to understand the seven steps your customers go through as they move closer and closer to making a final purchase decision. These steps exist in all sales environments, and are essential to the sales process. The seven steps of the buying cycle are:

**Step One: Need Identification.**
A need for a product or service is required to stimulate interest in making a purchase. Either your customer will have determined a need before they contact you — or you must help the customer realize they have a need.

**Step Two: The Search.**
Once a need is identified the customer starts to search for a source to satisfy their need. At this step it is most helpful to the customer, and most beneficial to you, to offer your customer two or three choices. (See Chapter 13)

**Step Three: A Source is Found.**
Once a search for a solution is started, eventually the customer will find a source that can satisfy their need.

**Step Four: Comparison.**

Although the customer has found a source to satisfy their need, they are unable to commit to a purchase. At this step they feel compelled to comparison shop. The customer may be satisfied to compare the current source to a product or service they've used in the past — or they may go somewhere else to find a similar product or service. Regardless of how they do it, most customers will insist on making a comparison before moving further along the buying cycle.

**Step Five: Decision Time.**

After making a comparison, the customer is usually confident enough to make a decision about a product or service — not necessarily a commitment — but a decision that may lead to a purchase.

**Step Six: Affirmation.**

After the customer has made a decision, typically they want to have it affirmed before making a purchase commitment. They need assurance that they are making the right decision. This is when salespeople must offer hard facts that affirm a purchase decision based on the benefits the customer will receive after the sale. You need to assure your customer that they are making the right choice.

**Step Seven: Relationship Established.**

To grow your business, this final step of the buying cycle is critical. Your customer must feel comfortable referring people to you — and returning to you to purchase other products and services. A relationship is based on how you relate with your customer. Without an established relationship your success in business will be tenuous.

Realize one sales transaction does not typically establish a relationship between you and your customer. Relationships typically happen when you — the salesperson — do something after the sale to create an ongoing need for your customer.

## LARGE SALE VERSUS SMALL SALE

Let's take a closer look at the difference between large and small sale environments, in terms of the buying cycle. In a large sale environment, each of the seven steps typically occurs during different contacts with your customer. Therefore, each step has to be managed more effectively. In a large sale environment it can be one or two weeks between contacts with your customer.

In contrast, in a small sale environment, three or four steps of the buying cycle can happen during your first contact with a customer. For example, a customer walks into a jewelry store, looks at some watches, compares a particular watch with other watches in the showcase, and then leaves to comparison shop.

Notice how many steps the customer went through during that first visit into the jewelry store. The challenge in a small sale environment is to determine how many steps happen during your initial contact, and to figure out how you will get the customer to return. How can you convince a customer to purchase your product or service before they leave the store?

There are three things to consider when you try to control the return of a customer. First is the frequency of the buy. How often will a customer most likely need to buy your product or service? Is it a consumable item or one that will last for a year, four years, or longer? Do you have vertical products or services they can buy from you? Can you create frequency around the product or service by offering add-on sales or services?

Second, what is the time line of the purchase? How much time usually occurs between the first contact you have with your customer and when they actually return to make a purchase?

Three, what is the time line to re-purchase? In your sales environment does a customer usually re-buy your product or service? Do they contract for a relationship or is the re-purchase a referral that they send to you? (Referrals are a continuation of the relationship you have established with your customer.)

*It's easier for your customer to make a final decision when smaller choices have already been made.*

## DEPENDENCY

Your challenge, then, is to create a dependency for your product or service. The most successful way to create a dependency is to be a specialist in your field or the industry in which your product is used. If you are a source of knowledge for your customer, they will depend on you for this information.

If you offer a service to monitor or service the products you sell, and your customers can't get this service anywhere else, you control the customer's buying cycle — solely from dependency.

## TAKE CONTROL

Some strategies that will help you control your customer's buying cycle are:

**Strategy 1: The Pre-Buy or Pre-Order Strategy**

Ask your customer for a pre-agreement during the early stages of the buying cycle. Let's say you have a customer who is at stage three of the buying cycle. They have found a source to satisfy their need. Even though they have not yet compared or affirmed their decision, ask them if they would consider buying your product — based on what it can do to satisfy their need. As you will learn, the key to getting a final yes from customers is to acquire a series of pre-agreements throughout the sales presentation.

**Strategy 2: The Order Form Strategy**

Imagine you have an order form. What does your customer need to decide as a function of placing the order? Early in the buying cycle move your customer into the choices they must make before they can actually make a final decision. For instance, if your product or service has many specifications, separate these into separate choices that lead toward a final decision. Your goal is to piece together the final decision, similar to piecing together a jigsaw puzzle. If the pieces fit (are agreeable to your customer) the sale works. It's easier for your customer to make a final decision when smaller choices have already been made. Be sure to discuss these little choices early in the sales cycle.

**Strategy 3: Contact Frequency**

It is imperative for you to increase the frequency of the contacts you have with your customers. If you work in a large sale environment you want to make sure that you keep the momentum of the buying cycle moving. One way to do this is to monitor the frequency of your contacts. If you make contact with a customer today — and you don't expect to talk with them again for a couple of weeks — reconsider if this length of time between contacts isn't too long. By placing this much time between contacts are you giving your customer the opportunity to see a competitor or to reconsider their purchase decision? Try to shorten the distance between contacts — without creating a high-pressure sales environment.

**Strategy 4: Timing Strategy**

You must be aware of where your customer is at in the buying cycle. If you don't know where they are, you stand a good chance of making an irrelevant sales presentation. This is called timing. By asking the right questions (see Chapter 8) you can determine their position.

> Sell Easy Example:
>
> You sell commercial clothes dryers (a large sale environment). A customer comes to you for a bid on fifty heavy-duty dryers, after they have already received three other bids. If you don't ask the right questions and discover this important piece of information at the start, you run the risk of losing any chance of making the sale. If you don't ask questions, you might base your presentation on the assumption that they haven't found a solution to their need for dryers, when in actuality they are coming to you for a price comparison or an affirmation of their decision. The timing of your sales presentation will be out of sync with where they are. You might be spinning your wheels trying to sell them on your dryers, not realizing the only reason they are checking with you is to validate a price they've already been quoted. Timing is essential. Ask questions.

## Strategy 5: Hard versus Soft Differentiators

To acquire business from customers it is necessary for you to explain the uniqueness of your product or service by using hard differentiators, as opposed to soft differentiators. A soft differentiator like "We have the best product on the market" has little impact. Doesn't everyone say this? However, a hard fact like "Ninety-nine percent of the time our product is dependable" differentiates your product from the competition. Few people can quote this rate of reliability.

Sometimes it is difficult to determine what is a soft differentiator and what is a hard differentiator. If you can quantify the unique benefits of your product or service usually you have moved into hard differentiators.

## SELL EASY RULES

**Rule Number One: Ask questions to determine what step of the buying cycle your customers are in.** Appropriate questions will generate the information you need. "How many products like this have you looked at already?" "When are you going to make a final purchase decision?"

**Rule Number Two: Seek your customer's preferences early.** Try to get a feel for what your customer needs at the start of your sales presentation. Once you acquire this understanding you will be able to work on getting pre-agreements throughout the rest of your sales presentation. Pre-agreements can prevent you from getting stalled later on. (See Chapter 14 )

**Rule Number Three: Establish a pattern of usage or consumption on the part of the customer.** If your customer is calling you to order something or to request service, you don't have control of your customer's buying cycle. When you contact them first and dictate the frequency of contact, then you have control of their buying cycle.

> Sell Easy Example:
>
> The dealer I purchased my automobile from keeps track of how often I drive 2,800 miles. From my records they can determine when my car needs to be serviced, and they call me to make arrangements to pick up my car from my home.

**Rule Number Four: Qualify total interest in the whole relationship, not just in the sale.** You must devise ways to keep your customer involved in a business relationship with you after the sale. Assure your customer that you are not going to disappear once the transaction is completed. Often times, a maintenance schedule can act as such a vehicle.

> Sell Easy Example:
>
> If you install residential HVAC systems, be sure that as a part of your sales presentation you demonstrate the benefits of regularly scheduled maintenance to keep a system in peak performance. Explain how your technicians monitor systems throughout the year by establishing a service contract with your customer.

Don't wait until your presentation is over and ask, "Oh. By the way, do you want a service contract?"

**Rule Number Five: Define the decision-making process.** Who is going to make the purchase decision? Are there multiple decision-makers or will you be dealing with only one purchaser? If there are multiple decision-makers you need to understand the roles that each will play in the purchase process.

# Turn Soft Differentiators
# Into Hard Differentiators:

Soft Differentiator:
We offer a one-year warranty program.
Hard Differentiator:
We offer a five-year parts and service warranty program.

Soft Differentiator:
Our technical support staff is available Monday through Friday, 8 to 5.
Hard Differentiator:
Our technical support staff is available seven days a week, with a guaranteed response time of sixty minutes.

Soft Differentiator:
We service the products we sell.
Hard Differentiator:
We have a fleet of servicemen on call twenty-four hours a day. They will respond to a service call within four hours.

Soft Differentiator:
We offer a regular maintenance program with every new vehicle we sell.
Hard Differentiator:
We offer a maintenance program with every new vehicle we sell, which includes pick up and delivery of the vehicle to and from your home, so you don't have to be without your car during the day.

Sell Easy Example:

In the retail furniture business it is common for one spouse to do the initial search, find, and decision making. Later, the other spouse visits the furniture store to reaffirm the decision (selection) of the other spouse. Your challenge is to understand the dynamics of all types of decision-making processes.

Once you begin to take control of your customer's buying cycle, you will make stronger sales presentations and have more success at growing your business.

## SELL EASY TIPS

◆ Understand the seven steps of the buying cycle: need identification, the search, a source is found, comparison, decision time, affirmation, and relationship established.

◆ Know the different buying cycles between large and small sale environments.

◆ Turn soft differentiators into hard differentiators.

◆ Always know where your customer is at in the buying cycle.

# PART II

## YOUR SALES PRESENTATION

# Chapter Six

# Start Your Day With a Bang

ALTHOUGH YOU HAVE A GREATER UNDERSTANDING OF YOUR CUS-
tomers and are better able to explain the uniqueness of your
product or service, unless your presentation is attractive, you
may never get your customers' attention and have the opportunity to sell to them. Today, packaging is key. And in sales,
that means presentation.

To understand the importance of presentation, walk into a
supermarket and look at the similar products on the same
shelf. Store brands mimic the packaging (presentation) of
national brands — in an attempt to lure customers to try
their products. It is the same with sales. Before you can
explain to your customers (and potential customers) why

they should do business with you and not someone else you must attract their attention with a quality presentation. Once your presentation is as polished, you'll get your customer's attention and be able to use the information you acquired in Part One.

In this part of the book I will discuss the important elements of a quality sales presentation.

What you do at the start of your workday and how you schedule various tasks throughout the day will determine the degree of success you achieve. You've heard people say, "I got up on the wrong side of bed this morning, and no matter what I tried to do, I couldn't seem to accomplish anything today." This is the same philosophy. How you start your workday is critical to your success.

Although each job requires different duties and responsibilities, almost all jobs encompass a combination of three different activity levels. The amount of concentration and effort required on your part varies with each activity level. The three activity levels are:

♦ Level one activities are tasks you perform to reach a particular result or goal.

♦ Level two activities are paperwork.

♦ Level three activities are tasks you don't *need* to do, but you do them as an escape or diversion from other activities.

To start your day with a bang and to be the most productive, you must schedule your activities to take advantage of your varying energy and concentration levels. Studies show that most workers focus better in the morning or at the beginning of their workday. A significant decrease in the ability to concentrate is experienced after lunch, and certainly by late afternoon. The human body naturally runs out of steam.

Therefore, to enjoy the most productive day possible it is imperative you begin your day by doing level one activities — when you are at your optimum performance level.

A **level one activity** is a results-oriented action. It is a core activity, like learning a new skill or talking on the phone with someone who might take advantage of your product or service. Getting information to a customer so they can make a decision in the short term, prospecting, and follow-up are also level one activities.

Paperwork of any sort is considered a **level two activity**. Making a list of people to contact during your level one activity time, completing files on your customers, or filling out order forms are level two activities. It is sometimes very easy for paperwork (a level two activity) to push into your level one activity time — to the point where you end up doing more paperwork than selling. Be aware of this phenomenon. Although you may find level two activities to be easier or more enjoyable, it is the level one activity that gets you to your goal of the final yes.

**Level three activities** are tasks you don't *need* to do, but you do them as an escape from performing level one or level two activities. For example, opening junk mail (don't take this personally if you're in direct mail marketing) tends to be a level three activity, even if you enjoy sorting through it. Because of their unimportance and low attention requirement, level three activities are best kept for the end of your workday — a time when you have less energy to concentrate on more important tasks.

## SELF-DISCIPLINE

To follow your daily work schedule you will need a certain amount of self-discipline. Without discipline it can be easy to perform level two or level three activities during your level one time.

Let's say you arrive at the office to start your day, and rather than making phone calls you gravitate to an inbox that's full of junk mail. Or you sit down and make a list of people you need to speak with that day, instead of already having a list prepared. At times like these you need to acknowledge that you've strayed from your level one activities and get back on track.

Sometimes, however, your environment can adversely affect your good intentions. In my position I am supposed to receive daily reports from several people before they leave the office each afternoon. I review their reports and provide feedback to them by noon of the following workday. Invariably there are days when I don't receive their reports until the next morning, during my level one time. In order to meet my noon deadline, I must review their reports immediately, which means that due to outside (environmental) influences, a different activity has been shifted into my level one time.

*Tasks or functions that are necessary to grow your business should be targeted as level one activities.*

In this type of situation, you must deal with the priority task at hand, then return to your level one activities as soon as possible. Try to avoid letting your environment disrupt the momentum of your workday.

> Sell Easy Examples:
>
> There is a yellow note sticky note by your telephone. It is a request for you to return a telephone call from a buyer. Even if this buyer is not a primary customer, the need to return the phone call is pressing — because the note is so visible. By its mere presence, the message has intruded into your level one time. Ignore the note until your level one tasks are completed.

> Paperwork can quickly accumulate and put pressure on your level one activity time. Things that are visible pile up, whether they are important or not. They call for your attention. This phenomenon is very true of paperwork. Beware! Ignore the stacks until an appropriate time in your workday. Avoid being sidetracked.

## SELL EASY RULES

**Rule Number One: Target core activities to heighten your results.** Target your level one activities to improve the results of your hard work. In my business, I need to prospect for new business. Therefore I spend twenty percent of my workweek looking for potential clients who have a high enough need for my product or service. I block this core activity into my schedule.

Since I also benefit from referrals, another core activity for me is to ask my current customers for names of people who they think might be interested in my services.

As a nontraditional salesperson you might spend a lot of

time solving problems. If this is the case, a core activity for you might be following up with a customer who needs help. Or if you rely on coworkers for support or information, a core activity for you could be to communicate with them on a regular basis.

**Rule Number Two: Define your best level one activities.** It is critical for you to define four or five core tasks each day so that when you have accomplished them you can say, "Wow! I've had a great day and it's only 10:00 a.m." I know that if I can reach four or five customers on the phone first thing in the morning, that sixty to seventy percent of the success of my day has already been established. I've started my day with a bang.

I realize that not every sales environment allows for this type of start. But, no matter what position you're in, there are things you can do at the beginning of your day to ensure your day is productive. If you do not define an activity you cannot benchmark your response in making your day start off with a bang. In order to feel accomplishment you must define your tasks.

**Rule Number Three: Create an environment that lessens the need for self-discipline.** People say to me, "Boy you have lots of self-discipline. Your business is so successful."

"Absolutely not," I reply. "I'm like every other person. I reach for the easiest thing there is to do. The main difference is I strive to make the critical tasks that I need to accomplish easy to do."

Sell Easy Example:

I used to love french fries, even though I know they are

unhealthy. When I get hungry while driving, I think about stopping off at a fast food restaurant for some fries. It's quick and easy. But, if there is a banana on the front seat of my car, I will reach for it, instead of pulling off and ordering my fries. Less self-discipline is required when the healthiest (most productive) choice is at hand.

If you know you have to telephone ten people first thing in the morning, you don't need a lot of self-discipline to make your business calls. All you need to do is make sure that your desk is empty — except for the list of people you need to contact. By making certain there is nothing to distract you or to get in your way, you reduce the need for great amounts of self-discipline.

I am not saying you don't need *any* self-discipline as you go through your day. What is important is making it easier to do the right thing rather than the easier thing (banana versus french fries). If you can do this you will have greater success at accomplishing the level one activities that are so necessary to succeed at your job.

### *Create an environment that lowers the pressure on self-discipline.*

**Rule Number Four: Accomplish level one activities during level one time.** Ask yourself "What is a level one activity?" Is calling someone on the telephone a level one activity? Is getting information for a customer who can make a buying decision by Friday a level one activity? Is compiling a list of people you can telephone or who you should see a level one activity? Is filling out a call report a level one activity — or is it a level two activity?

Sell Easy Example:

Many of my customers are easy to reach first thing in the morning. It is therefore most productive if I make telephoning a core activity — a level one activity — when my customers are available.

Establishing your level one activities is a challenge you will face daily. I look at level ones as core activities. For me, learning a new skill is a core activity. Therefore, I always try to schedule my training and education in the morning. If I learn a new skill in the morning, I can implement it immediately into my workday.

**Rule Number Five: Share your commitment with coworkers.** Tell other people in your office or department that you plan to be on the telephone (or whatever level one activity you have scheduled) from 8:30 a.m. until 10:00 a.m. If you are not on the phone between 8:30 a.m. and 10:00 a.m. your co-workers will say, "Hey, why aren't you in your office? It's nine o'clock and you're standing around chit-chatting at the water cooler." They will act as your conscious. They will prod you into accomplishing what you have said you would.

It is possible that some days you will feel justified talking in front of the water cooler instead of working at your desk. Here are some common excuses for this behavior:

**Excuse #1:** You forgot your list of people and phone numbers at home.

**Response:** You need to have more self-discipline.

**Excuse #2:** You've had a great week so far (it's only Wednesday) and you feel you deserve a break. You are taking a little time for yourself.

**Response:** Reward doesn't come in level one time. It comes in level two or level three time.

The need to perform level one activities during level one time is critical — because you are at your prime in level one time. More importantly, your clients may also be at their best during this period, which means that your net results are heightened. The opportunity for positive results is greater.

During the morning you might be able to reach more people who are receptive to you. Thus, if you call clients during their level one time, which is also your level one time, you won't have to be that good. In contrast, if you telephone them on a Monday morning, which is not their level one time, you will have to dial more numbers before you reach the same amount of people. This will take more energy, you will probably get lower net results — and it requires more self-discipline.

Not only must you be more effective at scheduling level one activities to meet your prime time you also need to consider the level one time of your customers. Then you need to compress everything that is possible into that time frame.

## SELL EASY APPROACH

Divide your day from start to finish by blocks of time, specifying what you will do in each time frame. For example, you'll make phone calls from 8:30 a.m. until 10:00 a.m. You'll be in the field from 10:30 a.m. until 3:30 p.m. You'll be in the office doing paperwork from 4:00 p.m. until 5:30 p.m.

Of course, you'll rarely have a perfect day. You know that. Other people will get in the way of your schedule. If, however, you haven't told others how you plan to spend your day, then it is partially your fault if you receive numerous inter-ruptions. Most people will respect the structure of your day. It is critical to let others know what your commitment is at different times of your workday.

I call that sharing your perfect day.

**Rule Number Six: Cluster your activities.** The easiest way to have a great day is do things that are similar in the same block of time. For example, if you're going to make a series of phone calls, make them consecutively. If you're going to write a series of letters, write them at the same time. The reason for this is when you compress the amount of time devoted to a single activity or a single function, you tend to heighten your quantitative results and increase your produc-tivity.

Sell Easy Examples:

If you need to telephone ten people, make your phone calls one after another. You will get more quantitative net results and more positive responses to your requests than you would if you split up the phone calls. If you make one phone call at 9:00 a.m., stop to do some paperwork, make another call at 10:00 a.m., stop to do more paperwork, make yet another phone call at 11:00 a.m., and then return to your paperwork, you will expe-rience a diminishing return on your efforts. Putting a level two activity (paperwork) next to a level one activ-ity (phone calls) tends to lessen the energy cycle that is needed to complete a task well.

Telemarketers are usually instructed to make a phone call and then to complete the paperwork on the call before moving onto their next phone call. After switching back and forth between the two activities for several hours, the telemarketers have stopped receiving positive functional responses. Whereas if the telemarketers had clustered their phone calls into a single time period and then clustered the follow-up paperwork into a specific time period, they would see greater net productivity. In actuality they could probably double their net results.

More than anything else, the momentum you bring to the start of your day will affect what you accomplish. Your first hour should be your best hour. Your ability to cluster activities and your ability to share your schedule with coworkers is vital to the success of your business.

Once you've become adept at scheduling your workday you can then concentrate on improving your presentation skills. The skills I will examine in the remainder of this section include effective use of the telephone, asking the right questions, and selling to your customer's needs.

*When you compress a similar activity into a single block of time your productivity tends to increase.*

## Sell Easy Tips

- ♦ Identify level one activities that are essential to your job.

- ♦ Use self-discipline to maintain your schedule of activities.

- ♦ Create your "perfect day" and use it as a guideline for determining your activity schedule.

# Chapter Seven

# EFFECTIVE USE OF
# THE TELEPHONE

ALTHOUGH THE TELEPHONE HAS BEEN IN USE FOR MORE THAN ONE hundred and fifty years, it is one of the most misused business tools today. When used inefficiently telephones can frustrate you and irritate your customer, thereby hindering the development of a business relationship.

When used effectively the telephone can be used to gather and share information and to establish and maintain relationships with your key customers.

By identifying the common roadblocks to effective telephone communication, you can avoid the frustration of misusing this vital business tool — and improve your effectiveness on the job. There are six common roadblocks that get in the way of successful telephone communication. The first roadblock is **poor timing**.

Maybe you've noticed that your customers are rarely available on Monday mornings. And if they are available, your conversations are typically short. However, when you telephone their offices on Wednesday mornings your customers are almost always available to talk with you and the conversations are not rushed. You seem to have more time to present your information and you feel as though the call was more beneficial — to you and your customer.

To have the greatest success with your customers it is essential for you to telephone them when their schedules allow them time to talk with you. Timing is everything. Be aware of your customers' work schedules and arrange your telephone calls accordingly.

A second roadblock is **poor attitude**. How many times have you received a phone call from a solicitor asking for a donation or a salesman trying to sell you something and you were certain they were reading from a script? There was no feeling of commitment to their cause. They spewed forth information in a monotone, as if they were trying to talk fast enough to prevent you from interjecting a no. They had a poor attitude.

When you make a phone call do not read from a script. Smile and exude enthusiasm for your product or service.

Your customer will sense your interest — even over the telephone — and respond positively.

A third roadblock to effective telephone use is having a **weak offer**. A successful salesperson will offer a customer something, even if it is only to send them information.

Provide an opportunity for the customer to say yes. Give them a reason to talk with you. If a valuable offer is not made, your phone conversation will terminate and so will the opportunity to form a business relationship.

Failure to have a **point of interest** (POI) is a fourth barrier. (Some people refer to this as an *angle*.) To successfully grab a customer's attention you must discuss an interest they have that is also related to your product or service. You must know something that is important to them.

> Sell Easy Example:
>
> A replacement window salesperson is trying to acquire business by making cold phone calls. His opening line is: "What kind of windows do you have?" More often than not he will meet with disinterest and rejection. He has not offered a point of interest. If, however, he would say, "My company is working with a number of people in your area to help them reduce their utility bills in the winter. I am calling to offer you a free analysis to determine how much heat is escaping through the windows in your home." Wow! Now the customer is interested in what this salesperson has to say — because the angle is on reducing heating costs and saving money — not buying windows. That is a point of interest. That is an angle.

Most consumers are more receptive to warm calls than they are to cold calls. You will have greater access to a person's time and interest if you know *something* about them. Even if you received his or her name from someone who knows someone else who gave them the customer's name and phone number...you can make it a warm call. You will know something that's unique to them. It could be as simple as knowing their company is large enough to benefit from your services — or that they have several children under the age of ten.

Anything you can do to change a cold call into a warm call will be to your advantage, because most cold calls usually meet with a customer's rejection.

**Lack of dialogue** is the fifth barrier to effective telephone communication. Dialogue is two-way conversation. Successful telephone communication requires that two people converse. One person cannot do all of the talking while the other person only listens.

Analyze your phone conversations. Do you allow your customers the opportunity to say more than yes or no infrequently during your monologue? If not, you aren't communicating effectively. To stimulate more dialogue in your phone conversations, ask your customers open-probed questions. (See Chapter 8)

*Contact strategy creates urgency.*
*It creates interest.*

The sixth roadblock is a **lack of sequential contact strategy**. In most sales environments you cannot telephone a customer once and expect to make a sale or establish a relationship. By using other methods of communication you can establish a contact strategy with each customer.

For instance, in addition to making a telephone call, you can fax your customer information to promote their interest in your product or service. Sometimes different modes of communication can be used in tandem, i.e., fax him the same point of interest you left on his voice mail.

What if a customer doesn't have time to talk with you on the telephone or they don't return your call according to the schedule you requested? Try other modes of communication. (See Rule Number Seven.)

## Structuring Your Telephone Message

To meet with the greatest amount of success your telephone conversation must be focused and organized. You should provide specific information to your customer and be prepared to answer questions. A structure that has proven to be effective in getting a positive response for me is:

1. Identify yourself when you make the call.
2. Give the reason for your call up front.
3. Propose your offer.
4. Verify the customer's need.
5. Respond to reluctance.
6. Get some kind of agreement.

When you telephone a customer you cannot afford to be elusive. An effective opening must stimulate the customer's interest so they will allow you the opportunity to make your presentation.

Sell Easy Example:

"Hello. This is Joe Wilson, vice president of Acme Bag Company. I am calling you because you're a premier traveler and we specialize in reducing the frustration of broken and damaged bags. Our company has a suitcase that is guaranteed to keep you satisfied for life. Do you have a couple of minutes?" *(The salesman has addressed steps one, two and three.)*

---

## ROADBLOCKS TO EFFECTIVE USE OF THE TELEPHONE

1. Poor timing

2. Poor attitude

3. Weak offer

4. No point of interest

5. Lack of dialogue

6. Lack of sequential contact strategy

---

"Yes," replies the customer.

"We would like to ship you one of our bags." *(The salesman has made his offer.)*

"If you like the bag, would you be interested in taking advantage of our lifetime guarantee on the bag? What this means is that we will continually repair or replace the bag at anytime for no additional cost to you."

*(Again, the customer will respond affirmatively. This is called yes momentum — getting agreement. He asked a question that can only be answered with a yes.)*

Then Joe says, "I'd like to ship this out to you today. You'll receive it in five to seven days."

"Well, I don't know," says the customer. "What if I don't like the bag when I see it?" *(Joe must now deal with the customer's reluctance.)*

"That's fine," Joe says. "You'll receive a shipping label and a tag with the luggage. If you don't like it, all you need to do is put the label on the box. We'll pay for the return shipping. There is absolutely no cost to you." *(He just handled the reluctance. Then he verifies again.)*

"When you get the bag take a good look at it because I'd like to call you the day after you receive it to get your opinion."

*The customer confirms he will be in the office to receive Joe's call. Joe has completed all six steps — easily.*

Effective telephone skills are attainable if you have an expectant attitude, work your numbers, have an organized message with a strong point of interest — and ask the right questions.

## SELL EASY RULES

**Rule Number One: Have an objective for every telephone call.** Before you telephone your customer you must know why you're contacting them. Are you calling to set up a meeting with them? Are you calling to verify what they need? Are you calling to gain their interest so you can send them information about your product or service?

You will not be able to determine a call's success or failure if you haven't established an objective prior to placing the call.

**Rule Number Two: Use a structured approach.** In order for customers to focus on what you're saying, your message must be organized and well structured. On the previous page I review the best structure for an effective telephone conversation. Use it.

**Rule Number Three: Build a strong point of interest.** To capture a customer's attention, especially over the phone when you have only your voice and attitude to sell for you, you must grab their interest with a strong point of interest. It helps if you know a little bit about your customer so that you can identify a POI.

> Sell Easy Example:
>
> I fly over a hundred thousand miles a year on commercial airlines. One of the biggest frustrations I have is with damaged luggage. I know that no matter how carefully the handlers treat my bags, I will have to replace my luggage within a year. My suitcases have never lasted longer than that. If a salesperson telephoned me and asked if I was interested in using a premium travel bag — one that would be replaced or repaired for the rest of my life, satisfaction guaranteed for no additional cost — would I be interested? Of course. His point of interest to me, a business traveler, is a suitcase that will always be in peak condition. He has my interest and I will ask, "How can I get one?"

**Rule Number Four: Provide choices to your customer.** It is easier for a customer to make a decision between two or three things than to choose between something and nothing. When you ask a customer to meet with you, give them a choice of days. You could say, "Mike, in the next couple of weeks I'm going to be in your part of the country. I'll be there on Thursday of next week and Friday of the following week. Which day is best for you to meet with me?" It's a lot easier for Mike to make a choice between two days than to give you a positive answer if you said, "I have to be in your area next Thursday. Can you meet with me then?" Be flexible. Give your customer a choice.

Likewise, it is easier for a customer to schedule a meeting

with you if you select two or three dates for them to choose from, instead of asking them, "When can you meet?" Busy people don't want to figure out when they're available. They want you to give them two or three dates they can check on their calendars.

*If you want customers to make a selection you must first give them a choice.*

**Rule Number Five: Use open-probed questions.** Open-probed questions create dialogue, an essential part of effective two-way communication. For instance, "What frustrations have you had with checking your bags in the past?" (Any frequent traveler could share many stories.) Or "What's the single most important challenge your company has in reaching its goals?" These types of questions should stimulate a response. (For more discussion on how to ask the right questions see Chapter 8.)

**Rule Number Six: Get little agreements along the way.** You want to make sure that your customer says yes throughout the phone conversation. By giving your customer the opportunity to agree with you, you're building stepping stones of understanding and forming a foundation on which to make a sale.

Sell Easy Example:

"Mr. Smith, have you been frustrated with checking your bags in the past?" If Mr. Smith travels frequently, he is going to say yes. "How many bags have you gone through in the last eighteen months?" Again, his answer will affirm that new bags are a reoccurring need.

By structuring your dialogue around your customer's point of interest and your product or service, you will establish solid groundwork for making a sale.

**Rule Number Seven: If you can't reach them by phone, fax them.** The nice thing about fax numbers is you can almost always get a fax number from a receptionist. A receptionist who has been instructed to screen incoming phone calls to the boss's office is much more willing to part with the boss's fax number. Why? Because a fax number is a receptionist's escape. The receptionist is following the boss's orders of screening phone calls yet at the same time placating a salesperson's desire for a line of communication to the boss.

> *Caution: Avoid sending volumes of information over the fax. If you are trying to make initial contact with a customer do not fax more than two pages. One of the pages should be dedicated to questions that spark their interest and the second page should state "this is why my company is important."*

More importantly, the fact that someone hasn't returned your phone call doesn't mean they aren't interested in talking with you. Many times a fax machine is a busy person's escape from the demands of the telephone. They can read a faxed message on their time — without a salesperson breathing down the receiver at them.

Additionally, by their nature, faxed messages have a sense of urgency. Therefore, if you design your message effectively, you can receive many positive results from a fax.

## SELL EASY APPROACH

At the bottom of your fax include a list of responses for the customer to respond to:

Please check one:

&#10065;   Sorry, I can't return your call today because I'm busy with a project. I do want to talk with you about your product. Please telephone me on:

_____

&#10065;   This is the wrong number to reach me at. Here's a number where you can reach me directly.

_____

&#10065;   The best day/time of the week to reach me is:_____

&#10065;   Sorry, I am not interested in your product at this time.

Additional memo: _____

**Rule Number Eight: Use voice mail to your advantage.** When used appropriately voice mail can enhance your sales presentation. It can get you to your goal faster. The key is to leave your point of interest on the customer's voice mail. If you leave only your name and phone number chances are very slim you will receive a return phone call from your customer. If, however, you include a point of interest, if you capture your customer's interest, if you get them excited about what you have to say — then they will be more likely to return your call.

Voice mail can be used to create interest and re-affirm a point of interest with your customer. Two voice mails can set up an appointment. Instead of playing telephone tag, leave a message on your customer's voice mail that says, "I'm going to be available three times next week to discuss our offer. Leave a message on my voice mail and let me know which time is best for you to meet and I'll set our appointment for that day." After you receive a response on your voice mail, the appointment is set.

The avoidance of human contact is sometimes odd — but if you use fax machines and voice mail to their best advantage they can save you time — and they work.

**Rule Number Nine: Work the numbers.** If I sit down at my desk to telephone ten potential customers typically I will reach three of them. I know this to be true because I've spent twenty years doing it. Therefore, if I want to reach nine people in one week I need thirty names to call. If I'm fortunate, I may not have to contact all thirty people — but the key is that in order to reach nine customers I must prepare a list of thirty people to telephone. That is my 10-3-1 system.

From my sales experience I know if I talk to ten people I'll be able to interest three of them in my offer, and within five to six months, a fourth will become a customer. On the other hand, if I sit down with only five names to call, I won't reach anyone. The secret for me is to telephone ten people. The synergy will only work if I have clustered the names to work my formula. If I have a shorter list I lose my momentum and I don't make my goals.

If you pay attention to your numbers, you will find a formula that works for you. This is the formula you need to follow when structuring your daily activities. (See Chapter Six.)

When you get into structuring your dialogue, you can combine some of these strategies together to be more effective on the phone.

## Sell Easy Tips

♦ Have an objection for each telephone call you place to your customers.

♦ Avoid reciting a monologue — keep the conversation moving in two directions.

♦ Ask questions to generate responses from your customers.

♦ Turn cold calls into warm calls by knowing something about the person you are calling.

# Chapter Eight

# ASK THE RIGHT QUESTIONS

ONE OF THE MOST IMPORTANT RESPONSIBILITIES SALESPEOPLE have is to ask customers the right questions at the right time. It doesn't matter if a salesperson is talking with a customer over the phone or in person. To gain the information they need to help their customer purchase their product or service — they must ask specific questions.

There are two reasons to question a customer: to obtain soft facts and to obtain hard facts. **Soft fact questions** are general in nature. They relate to the qualitative relationship a customer has with your product. When you ask soft fact questions you can establish a relationship with your customer more easily than if you only ask them hard fact questions. Examples of soft fact questions are:

- ◆ "How do you feel about this?"
- ◆ "What experiences have you had before?"
- ◆ "Who are you currently buying from?"
- ◆ "What services are you using?"
- ◆ "How do you feel about that?"

A **hard fact question** is a qualifying question. They are usually quantitative: how many, when, where? Examples of hard fact questions are:

- ◆ "How many of these do you want?"
- ◆ "What is your budget?"
- ◆ "When do you need it?"
- ◆ "Who is going to help you make the purchase decision?"

Sometimes it is difficult for salespeople to ask soft fact questions. Rather than taking the time to establish a relationship with their customers, they move directly into hard fact questions.

The key to success in business is to ask your customers both soft fact and hard fact questions. It is best to begin a conversation with soft fact questions, since they create a relationship environment. Then, once you've built a foundation, ease into the hard fact questions to acquire specific information about the transaction you're trying to complete.

If you find yourself meeting with resistance or the conversation has stalled, ask your customer some soft fact questions. You will find that you can usually repair and strengthen the bonding process by returning to soft fact questions.

## PHRASING QUESTIONS

The way you phrase questions has a lot to do with the amount of information or resistance you receive from your customers. There are several ways to phrase questions. An **open-probed question** (many people refer to these as open-ended questions) begins with who, what, where, when, why and how. Questions like, "How soon do you need it?" "What experiences have you had in the past?" "When are you planning to take advantage of this product or service?" "Who will be making the final purchasing decision?" are open-probed questions. They usually generate the most detail from your customer.

Too often sales people ask **closed-probed questions** like, "Can we get together this week?" or "Does this fit into your budget?" These questions typically generate a single-word response, yes or no. Closed-probed questions do not encourage your customer to share information.

Additionally, when you ask closed-probed questions you put your customer in a high-pressure situation by anchoring them to a psychological or verbal commitment. For example, if you ask a customer, "Can we get together next Monday?" you are pressuring them to commit to a specific time. If, instead, you had asked, "What works best for you, Monday or Wednesday of next week?" there's less pressure for a definitive reply. They can be more flexible in their response. A softer question meets with less resistance.

**Tie-down** is a third way to phrase a question. With tie-downs you make a statement while anchoring the customer's agreement. For instance, "This is an important product to you because of your environment, isn't it?" You've made a value judgment and asked for their agreement, rather than asking a question and waiting for their response. A tie-down gives you the chance to make a presumed statement.

An advantage to tie-down questions is they too elicit important information from customers. If you make a statement like, "The price of this equipment isn't as important as the return on your investment, right?" Your customer might respond, "I don't know. We're really looking at price." By this response you now know where they stand. You know price is important to them.

Tie-down questions are essential in getting a yes from your customers in a closing situation. When people look at a salesman and say, "Gee, they're high pressure" or "You know, I really didn't enjoy that experience," it's usually because the salesperson waited until the end of the presentation before getting any verbal agreement from the customer. With tie-down questions a salesperson can get verbal agreements throughout their conversation — not just at the end.

"You will be making the final decision, won't you?" or "This decision will be made in the next four to five days, won't it?" are tie-downs that should be posed at some point during your presentation. To avoid surprises at closing, give your customer the opportunity to say yes or no — before you try to close. You don't want to make statements at closing that you hope are true.

---

### DIFFERENCES BETWEEN OPEN-PROBED AND CLOSED-PROBED QUESTIONS.

| CLOSED-PROBED QUESTION | OPEN-PROBED QUESTION |
|---|---|
| "Could we meet tomorrow?" | "How soon would it be convenient for you to meet with me?" |
| "Do you want me to get back with you next week? | "Is Tuesday or Thursday best for me to call you with information about this project?" |
| "Does your budget allow for this expense? | "Where can we meet to review your needs? |

---

The fourth way to phrase a question is called **volley**. Actually there are two kinds of volley questions. One is a **reverse back**, which means you reverse back a statement your customer has made as a question. Your customer says, "We're not going to be making a decision this week." Your reply is, "You're not going to be making a decision this week?" The volley puts the customer in the position of having to respond to you. It is a subtle way of asking your customer to validate what they said.

The other way to volley is to do a **question for question**, which is nothing more than eliciting an open-probe. For example, your customer says, "We weren't planning on making a decision right away." Your response is, "When are you planning to make a decision?" Or a customer says, "The price of your product is a little high." Your response is, "What are your budget restrictions?"

Volley is critical because it forces the customer to share information about their wants and needs, and makes them validate their position. Using volley questions keeps you from being on the defensive, especially when you are ready to close.

Effective questioning is essential if you are to establish a solid business relationship with your customers. Following are three rules of conversation to help you be more successful at interviewing your customers.

## SELL EASY RULES

**Rule Number One: Ask more questions than you make statements.** Salespeople are information burdened. Most of the training sales people receive relates to the features of their products and services. Thus sales people are very good at telling customers everything they know about their product. And, since customers ask questions about your products and services, it is easy to expound on the features of what you're trying to sell while neglecting to ask your customer questions.

I have been with salespeople who didn't pause once while they spewed forth their product information — and they were very proud of the fact they could recite their monologue nonstop. But what information did they learn about their customer? Salespeople who do not ask questions will have difficulty in servicing their customers well.

**Rule Number Two: Integrate questions that result in positive responses.** As you share facts about your product or service ask your customer questions to encourage their agreement. For example, you might say, "One of the benefits we bring to this environment, Nancy, is that we create a long, steady relationship with our customers so we can provide constant service to them. Is this kind of service important to you?"

By using this style of questioning you've converted a piece of information about your service into a question. You've gotten a tie-down before moving forward.

Very simply, if you ask your customer several anchored questions during your presentation, you will have a foundation of positive responses you can fall back on. Let's say you've received three pre-agreements from your customer — and then suddenly they disagree with something you've said. Rather than having to work very hard at overcoming this objection, you can easily remind them of their previous agreements, thereby returning to a more positive atmosphere.

*Asking the right questions is not just having the right questions to ask, but being able to ask them at the right time to build a foundation for a positive relationship.*

## SELL EASY APPROACH

Before asking a customer to make a decision — to answer a question — be prepared for their response. Let's say you asked a customer to buy your product. They say, "Yes, I'd like 500 items delivered by Friday." If you don't know if 500 is a quantity you can supply or that Friday is a feasible delivery date, what are your options?

There are two ways you can handle this situation. You can use this as an opportunity to verify their need by replying, "If I can deliver 500 by Friday you will place the order?" You are anchoring their business.

Your second choice — and this situation is not conducive to making sales — is to stall them by saying, "I don't know if we have 500. I have to check and get back to you later."

Be sure to have the appropriate information to take an order.

**Rule Number Three: Put power in your pauses.** Pauses are powerful. The ability to have a customer respond to a question because you're capable of dealing with a pause is almost as important as your questions. Unfortunately many salespeople don't do this. They fear silence.

When they ask a customer a question, they don't give the customer time to answer, and actually leap in with the answer themselves.

This type of behavior can prevent you from learning valuable information about your customer. Learn to pause after asking a question. Then you will be able to hear your customer's response.

## SELL EASY TIPS

♦ Understand the different approaches to asking questions.

♦ Build a list of questions that can be asked at different stages of the buying cycle.

♦ Gain a level of confidence by asking authoritative questions.

Chapter Nine

# DISCOVER YOUR CUSTOMERS' NEEDS AND WANTS

TO MAINTAIN AND INCREASE YOUR MARKET SHARE YOU MUST DIS-
tinguish yourself as a salesperson who satisfies his customers' needs and wants. You might have a unique product
and provide reliable service, but if you don't determine and
thereby satisfy your customers' needs and wants you won't
keep their business.

By interviewing your customers — asking them the right
questions — you can learn about their needs and wants. All
customers have needs and wants. And, to establish a quali-

ty, long-lasting relationship with your customers you must satisfy their needs and wants.

A need is something basic. "I need a computer." "I need a car."

A want is more detailed. "I want a fast computer." "I want a sports car."

You will not get your customers' attention if you sell only to their needs. Lots of people sell computers and cars. If, however, you address their wants for a *faster* computer or a *sporty* car, you'll be successful in getting their attention.

There are four steps to follow to determine a customer's needs and wants. First you must understand their **current situation**. What does the customer currently have? Where are they now? Questions like "What do you use now?" or "How long have you had it?" will stimulate the responses you need from a customer.

Second, by **identifying problems** your customer may have, you can focus on their needs and wants. Questions like "What problems are you experiencing?" or "Why are you considering a change?" or "Who has been servicing your current equipment?" can help identify a problem area. Furthermore, when a customer shares a problem with you they are letting you know what needs are not being satisfied.

Third, it is important for you to know what **implied effect** your customer anticipates he will get by purchasing your product or service. In other words, if you ask, "How will this product or service help you?" or "What cost benefit do you see by making this change?" you're going to learn what the customer expects your product or service will do for them.

Sell Easy Example:

A customer wants a computer with more memory. You could say, "Sue, if I increase your computer to thirty-two megabytes of RAM, how will that affect your business?" Sue might respond, "Well, I'll gain more processing speed, which will make my employees a lot happier. Right now they have to wait for their computers to process information. Then they become frustrated. Hopefully adding more RAM will significantly reduce the processing speed."

Sue's implied effect is happier and less frustrated employees.

The fourth step is **benefit verification**. When you discuss a benefit of your product or service with your customer you want them to say agree that the benefit is important to them. If they don't say it's important, you haven't verified the benefit.

In Sue's case it is processing speed. "Sue, would it be useful to you, if in addition to giving you thirty-two megabytes of RAM we also added new software to your system? This software is designed to streamline your type of work."

If Sue hasn't agreed this benefit is important, you don't have an anchor to return to if she hesitates. You can't go back and say, "You agreed speed was important, didn't you, Sue?" If you haven't established an anchor by verifying a benefit you may have to go through your entire presentation again — even in a closing environment.

Before you can close the transaction you need to reach this level of benefit verification. In other words, "Speed is important to you, right, Sue?" or "Driving a sports car and having that kind of fun feel on the road is important to you, isn't it?"

Samples of leading questions to get benefit verification:

♦ "Would it be beneficial for you to work with someone who knows what your future needs are, so that your needs can be satisfied quickly?"

♦ "If we knew that next month you would need this particular item, we could pre-order it for you so that it would be available for you immediately. Would this be a valuable service to you?"

♦ "How important is it for you to drive a car that makes a statement of style?"

Sell Easy Example:

Let's say you're in the personnel business. One of your customers periodically needs a temporary person to help them with a special project. You say, "Martha, if we knew what growth demands you expected in the next twelve to eighteen months, we could search for people with that kind of talent now. Then we would be ready to supply your need within twenty-four hours. Given your urgency and varying cycles, would this be important to you?" That is a benefit verification statement.

## MOTIVATION AND URGENCY

The key to exciting a customer is to establish their specific want, not just their need. By doing so you will heighten their motivation to buy.

Motivation is why your customer is considering a purchase. Without motivation a customer will not buy.

Urgency is the when; it is the buying cycle. Above all else, the urgency factor tends to support the buying cycle.

Even if a definable need exists and there is a level of motivation to make a purchase, without an urgency to buy, the entire sales presentation can be fruitless. If necessary, you must create urgency for the purchase of your product or service. The urgency could be as simple as the value your customer will gain by using your product or service. (See Chapter Ten.)

## SELL EASY RULES

**Rule Number One: Ask specific *want* questions.** Your questions should relate to a preference, not to a need. If you are satisfying your customers' needs but have not been successful in sales could be that you haven't discovered their wants. You're probably not getting to the want level because you aren't asking want-related questions like, "What specific features would you like on your mower?" or "What problems have you had with your current mower?"

If you discover a problem your customer has, oftentimes the problem in and of itself will indicate your customer's want. For example, if a customer tells you, "You know, from time to time I need a certain person to do a specific job. Whenever I call our employment firm, they don't have the kind of skilled person I need." Your customer's need to have the person is not the problem. That is not why your customer is considering making a change in employment agencies nor is it what they want to buy from you. This customer wants to work with a personnel agency that has the type of skilled people he needs — when he needs them.

So you move to implied effect. And that is, "In other words, what you're telling me, Mike, is it's important to you for us to preplan your needs so we are ready for you when you call us."

Then you go to benefit verification. "What you're looking for is an agency that has this kind of skilled person available on a short-notice. Is that what you're telling me?" What you will get from this question is an anchor.

> Sell Easy Examples:
>
> A customer says, "I need a riding lawn mower. I want a mower that has a service program to guarantee I'll always have a mower to use, even when mine is in for repair. I want to be able to mow my grass at any time."
>
> This customer is not only buying a mower; he is buying the assurance that he will always have a mower available.
>
> ~
>
> A customer needs a watch. She wants a watch that shows the date. A good salesperson will sell the benefit of a particular watch based on the fact it has a clearly stated date on its face.
>
> The customer could buy any watch but it's the value of satisfying her want for a date that she will pay for.

In almost any environment, as soon as you sell to a want, the pressure on price is lessened. The customer will pay more to satisfy a want. Doug might pay $25,000 for an automobile, but if it's a sports dynamic he'll pay more. The car might be getting smaller but the sporty design is more important to him.

*Success in selling depends on your ability to establish your customers' wants, to verify the benefit of their want, and to anchor their agreement to the importance of satisfying that want.*

**Rule Number Two: Isolate your customer's most important want.** Determine the highest want of your best customer and satisfy it. Design your presentation around satisfying your customer's highest want.

> Sell Easy Example:
>
> When a couple takes their toddlers to dinner, their need is food. But speed and ease is their want. Their want for fast, easy service supercedes their need for food. The couple will drive up to a window. It's fast. The kids love the toys. The kids will be quiet.

**Rule Number Three: Sell to your customer's wants by defining three things your product or service will do for them.** Once you establish your customer's wants you must state three ways your product or service satisfies those wants.

> Sell Easy Examples:
>
> Doug wants a sports car. During your presentation identify three things about a particular car that will satisfy his need for a sporty car. One is design. Two is the way the car handles the road. And three is the car's color. It will be easy for Doug to say yes, yes, and yes.

> Sue wants a faster computer. During your presentation explain how your computer will allow her employees complete their jobs faster and more efficiently. Discuss how her employees will be happier using the new equipment, and how fewer problems will arise while they process the jobs, especially when they're under a lot of pressure. These are three reasons for Sue to say yes, yes, and yes.

## SELL EASY TIPS

♦ Understand the difference between needs and wants.

♦ Ask questions to discover your customers greatest wants.

♦ Identify at least three ways in which your product or service satisfies your customer's greatest wants.

♦ When you satisfy your customer's wants the pressure on price decreases.

Chapter Ten

# SELL VALUE — NOT PRODUCT

THE DEMAND OF TODAY'S MARKETPLACE IS TO PRICE YOUR PROD-
uct or service at a level that is comparable to your competitors' products and services. If you want to charge a premium
price, you must convince your customers of the value of your
product. Before a customer will pay a premium price, they
need to understand what unique value you offer. What value
is uniquely yours?

Value is what sets your product apart from your competition. Salespeople say, "Our product has a lot of value" or
"Our service is valuable." If, however, you are unable to
define your product's value you won't be able to sell your
product — your package.

That's right. Value must be packaged. Value must be a tangible component of your product or service.

Can you get the product to your customers in twenty-four hours or less? Do you deliver your service in a unique environment? What do you do or have that is unique? You must promote your uniqueness to distinguish your company or yourself in the market — something all business people must do to succeed.

> Sell Easy Example:
>
> The service contract I received when I purchased my car includes a 2,800-mileage care package. Every 2,800 miles the dealer retrieves my car from my garage, takes it to the service center, has it serviced, and then delivers it back to my garage before I need it the next morning. I am not aware of another dealership in my area that offers this service. This service contract is my dealer's category authority. It is their uniqueness — and it is a feature that is valuable to me.

## ESTABLISHING VALUE

**Define your value.** Value can be many things, but it must be defined. Value must be responsive to your customer's needs, and it must be convenient. Remember in Chapter Two you determined your category authority. Your category authority is what makes your business is number one at. It might be the technical capability of your people. It might be the ability you have to respond to your customers in a short period of time.

Maybe its the quality of your product. Is quality defined in terms of the durability of your product or the quality of your service?

The service I get from my car dealer— the value component — is that I don't have to hassle with arranging for trans-
portation to and from the service center. This is a definable
value.

> Sell Easy Example:
>
> An HVAC company sells comfort to their customers. The
> company supports their customers with a fleet of service
> technicians who are available twenty-four hours a day.
> In addition to scheduling regular maintenance checks,
> the company responds to service calls within four
> hours. The HVAC company ensures that their cus-
> tomers' businesses or homes are at the comfort level
> they need. That's definable. It's value.

**Response.** To establish value, your response time in satisfying your customers' needs is critical. My dealer monitors
my driving habits. They have a software program to determine when I have driven 2,800 miles -and they call me when
my car needs to be serviced. What a great value this is. They
monitor my comfort so I don't have to. They respond before
I know I need them. It's the response that attracts me to this
car dealer.

**Convenience.** It must be convenient for your customers to
use your product or service. It's not what the feature is — it's
what the feature does for the customer. What is the convenience to your customer?

In the example of the service agreement I have on my car,
the underlying benefit is that within reason I will always have
a car to drive. The dealer services my car at night. It is very
convenient for me.

Sell Easy Example:

Dentist Smith has evening hours two nights a week, plus every Saturday morning. Dentist Jones is not open in the evenings and is only open one Saturday morning a month. Which dentist is most convenient to people who work eight to five, Monday through Friday?

## PRICE AND VALUE

Price is a reflection of value. It does not stand alone. The value of what you deliver takes the pressure off of the price you charge. If your product or service rates high in terms of quality, response, and convenience the pressure to keep your price low is removed. You can raise your price above a competitor who does not offer the value that you do.

Sell Easy Example:

Although I do not pay for the pick up and return of my car — I am certain I pay a premium price for the work the dealer performs on my car once it is in the shop. I don't mind paying a little more for the work — because the value of the service is worth any extra they charge.

## SERVICE AND VALUE

Service is a component of value, although, it too must be defined. I'll give you an example. While travelling on business in Florida I went into a grocery store to purchase some toiletries. At the checkout counter I asked the cashier, "Can I write a check?"

"Sure," she said. "We look forward to serving people who use checks. Are you from the area?"

"No. I'm from Minneapolis."

"Oh, great. What are you doing in Orlando?" (This is called relationship building.) I tell her I'm in town on business.

"Mr. Winninger," she says as I'm leaving, "thank you for shopping at our grocery store."

"How did you know my name?" I ask.

"It's on your check."

These are definable services: bonding with a customer, developing a relationship, and using the customer's name.

> *If you can't define the service, it*
> *isn't a value component.*

## FEATURE, ADVANTAGES, AND BENEFITS

A **feature** is something that is offered by your product or service. One of the features of the grocery store was that they accepted personal checks.

**Advantages** are general. They are available to all customers. This store accepted personal checks from all of their customers.

**Benefits**, on the other hand, are specific to individual customers. I personally benefited from being able to write a check while travelling out of town on business. It was convenient for me. They made me feel at home in Orlando.

## SELL EASY APPROACH

A successful sales person will take their customers through the three levels of value.

1.  Feature is.

2.  Advantage does generally for anybody.

3.  Benefit is specific to each customer.

Benefits are critical in satisfying a customer's needs and wants. To increase your value you must determine your customer's wants and satisfy them. (See Chapter Nine.)

Sell Easy Examples:

Let's return to car sales. A young woman is shopping for a sports car. Instead of highlighting the design features of a particular sports car, let her know what the car will do for her. "After driving conventional automobiles for years, imagine the fun you will experience by driving this car." Make driving the sports car personal to your customer. It isn't a sports car just sitting on the floor. Share how dynamic and alive she will feel driving the car.

You're going to sell a customer a piece of equipment. The advantage to this piece of equipment is its durability. It will get the job done consistently, for anyone, for a long period of time. The specific benefit to your customer is that due to their short-term demands, you guarantee to provide this piece of equipment to them when they need it. It now becomes important to your customer to work with you.

Typically most salespeople stop at the advantage level and fail to get specific with each customer. Remember: it's truly benefits that sell value to your customer.

♦   Benefits solve problems. What's your customer's problem? Your customer calls and wants a piece of equipment tomorrow. You have the equipment they need.

♦ Benefits support price. If a customer makes short-term demands you can charge more for the fast turn around. There is value in your service.

♦ Benefits develop uniqueness in your product. The uniqueness comes from the fact that to a customer a certain feature is specific to them, even if it is available to a lot of people. The uniqueness becomes tangible.

♦ And finally, benefit gives motive. If you can show your customers the benefits they will receive from your product or service they will have a reason — a motive — to buy.

*The closer a customer feels the advantage of a feature is to them, the more likely they are to buy your product or service.*

## SELL EASY RULES

**Rule Number One: Verify the importance of your customer's want.** After determining your customer's wants and needs verify their importance. And help prioritize their needs and wants.

**Rule Number Two: Anchor a value that is tied to your customer's highest want or need.** Find a value of your product or service that relates to your customer's highest want, then anchor an agreement to that value.

**Rule Number Three: Share three benefits that satisfy your customer's wants.** Define three things your product does from a benefit standpoint for your customer. By doing this you will take pressure off your price and distinguish yourself from the competition. Your customer will focus on you and your product.

> *The number of benefit statements used by a sales professional directly equates to more successful closings.*

**Rule Number Four: Share more benefits about your product or service than you do features.** Often salespeople become so involved in explaining the features of their products they inundate their customers with information that isn't specific to the customer's priorities. It isn't the quantity of features you share about your product that garners successful closings. What works, according to a survey by Michigan State University, is the number of benefit statements you share with a customer. The more benefits you state, the greater your chances for a successful closing.

## REVIEW

You know that planning your daily activities, using the telephone effectively, and asking your customers the right questions will stimulate communication with your customers, to the point where you can discover their needs and wants. You also know that by matching the value of your product or service to these needs you will have a good base for a strong and effective sales presentation.

However, in order to get the yes you desire from your customers, you must also have functional responses at the tip of your tongue and know how to overcome resistance. These are skills that will be addressed in Part Three, "Getting The Yes."

## SELL EASY TIPS

♦ Identify the difference between features, advantages, and benefits.

♦ Focus your presentation on the benefits of your product or service — in relation to your customer's greatest needs and wants.

♦ Value is what sets your product or service apart from the competition.

# PART III

## GETTING THE YES

# Chapter Eleven

# CHARACTERISTICS OF A SUCCESSFUL CLOSER

TO SUCCEED IN SALES YOU MUST BE SKILLED AT MANY THINGS. YOU have to effectively identify your customer's needs. Do they want a car that is economic — or a car that gives them prestige? You need to identify and take control of their buying cycle. When do they need the car? Are they just looking or must they purchase a car by the end of the month? You need to be good at explaining your uniqueness and the value of your product. What specific things will your product or service provide to your customer? How will your customer benefit?

And, of course, you have to be skilled at closing the transaction.

Being a successful closer is more than getting your customers to say yes *at the end* — it is the process of getting agreements from your customers many times *throughout* your sales transaction. Closing consists of two stages.

The first stage is called **affirmation**. That's when your customer agrees to little things that can lead to a final decision. For example, "Joe, do you like the service feature of this program?" instead of, "Joe, do you want to sign-up for the program?" Before you ask your customer to buy the whole program, get affirmations on some of the features or benefits. Even when a customer agrees on a particular color or style, you're getting an affirmation.

The second stage is called **confirmation**. Confirmation is the final agreement. It's when you ask the customer to commit to making the purchase.

Affirmation and confirmation go hand in hand. You can't separate one from the other. Affirmations lessen the pressure on the customer and thereby increase the probability that they will say yes. Typically, if a salesperson is a successful closer, he or she is skilled at getting agreements from their customers throughout the sales transaction. Additionally, successful closers understand the importance of the following five elements.

### 1. Timing.

Closing is the end result of the affirmations you've accumulated during your presentation. If you try to close too soon or without any affirmations, you could miss out on some information that is important for the sale to go through. Without this information your timing will be off, and you stand a greater chance of failing to get the final commitment. In contrast, talking too much can affect your timing. Have you ever received so much information from a salesperson that you walked away without making a purchase? They talked beyond the point of closing. Poor timing.

Sell Easy Example:

Speed (or lack of) in service can affect the timing of a sale. I'm sure you've stood in a slow-moving line in a retail shop, eventually lost interest and/or patience — and left the store without purchasing the item that was in your hand. You didn't walk away because you didn't want the product — you walked away because the opportunity to purchase the product went beyond the opportunity of saying yes. The sale was lost due to slow timing.

## 2. Identify the highest needs of your customer.

It is critical to establish your customer's highest needs so that you can anchor your closing to them. (See Chapter Nine.) If you don't know what is most important to your customer, you will probably lose their interest.

Sell Easy Example

A customer looking for an easy-to-use camera visits a camera shop. The salesperson in the shop immediately directs the customer's attention to the newest digital camera, and begins talking about the advanced features of the camera. The customer walks away, dissatisfied, because the salesperson failed to identify their need for a camera that was simple to operate.

*Caution: Beware of selling the features you think are most attractive about your product or service. Listen to what your customer needs — then focus on the features that satisfy those needs.*

### 3. Ask appropriate questions.

To steer your customer in the direction of a buying decision, it is necessary for you to ask effective questions. Before you reach the end of your presentation you should have asked your customer several questions to initiate a buying decision. Examples of buying-type questions are:

♦ "Do you want two or three widgets?"

♦ "Do you want this in red or yellow?"

♦ "Do you need it delivered tomorrow or next Monday?"

♦ "Do you prefer a sixteen-by-twenty-inch photo or a twenty-by-twenty-four-inch photo?"

♦ "Where do you plan on displaying this sculpture?"

The most important thing these types of questions do is they get your customer imagining what it would be like to purchase and use your product or service.

### 4. Ask for the final agreement.

A surprising number of salespeople don't ask for a yes before they pull out the purchase agreement or the contract. This high-pressure environment will almost always result in a failure to close.

Sometimes salespeople don't ask for a final agreement because they assume they have the sale — or they fear rejection. The salesman hopes that if he assumes he has the sale, he will get it. This type of logic rarely works.

Remember the saying, you can't get what you don't ask for. Get verbal affirmations up front, before you move into a contract situation. Affirmations let you know if your customer is ready to make a final decision.

When customers say they aren't ready to make a decision use the opportunity to find out why they aren't ready. Simply ask, "Why? Why are you reluctant to make a decision?" or "What is keeping you from going ahead with the purchase?" Their answers can help you determine what you've missed as far as relating the value and benefits of your product or service to their greatest need.

**5. Avoid responding to too many objections.**

It is possible for salespeople to spend time responding to so many objections they can't conclude their presentation. If you handle an objection to price; then an objection to color, and then to quantity, etc., you could begin to feel like a tennis ball bouncing back and forth against a wall. Don't get stuck responding to an onslaught of objections. This stalls the sales process. Time and energy are spent. A successful close needs momentum.

## SELL EASY RULES

**Rule Number One: Ask strong ownership questions.** Encour-age your customer to visualize how it would feel to use the product or service you're selling. Examples of ownership questions are:

- ◆ A real estate agent asking a client how they would decorate a particular room

♦ A physical trainer asking a client about their energy levels throughout the day

♦ A lawn mower salesman asking questions about a customer's yard

♦ A computer salesman asking what type of analysis or database is needed

These questions relate to usage. They help customers take psychological possession of the product or service.

**Rule Number Two: Anchor value to your customer's highest need.** When you question your customer, your goal should be to find the one thing — more than anything else — that they need or want. Going back to the customer who wanted a camera that was simple to operate. The customer was not interested in plugging a camera into his computer and sending photos via the Internet to his family and friends. He simply wanted a camera that was easy to use.

Unfortunately, many salespeople try to sell based on their opinion rather than their customer's need — and they miss the close.

> Sell Easy Example:
>
> Hertz discovered that the highest need for most business travelers was to get to their destination quickly. So Hertz promoted its fast service and succeeded in addressing the highest need of most travelers. Hertz's ability to satisfy this need also took the pressure off of price and made it easier for the traveler to commit to Hertz — because their highest needs were being met.

**Rule Number Three: Listen to what is *not* said by your customer.** Watch your customer's body language. If the customer leans back and crosses his arms, you're not relating to him. You are failing to address the issues he feels are important. In contrast, if your presentation addresses his needs, the customer will show interest in what you're saying.

**Rule Number Four: Isolate real resistance.** It is critical for you to isolate why your customer is reluctant to make a purchase decision and to validate their reason. Maybe they aren't in a position to make the final decision. Maybe other people are involved. Maybe they haven't compared you to anyone else yet. Everyone wants to compare before making a commitment to buy. (See Chapter Five.) Set yourself up as a comparison by offering two or three choices to your customers. (See Chapter Thirteen.) This strategy can prevent your customer from feeling the need to go into the market to find a comparison.

**Rule Number Five: Have a positive attitude.** You don't have to be motivational — but be positive. Look for good things to happen. Have an expectant attitude. Anticipate that there is something about your product that relates to most people you talk with. Concentrate on the unique qualities of your product that suit each customer's needs. This doesn't guarantee that all of your customers will purchase your product or service, but an optimistic and positive attitude makes the environment more pleasant — for you and for your customers.

In other words, when you meet with a customer, expect that there is something about your product or service that is of interest to them. Find out what they are interested in and relate that to your product. Build your presentation around this.

And never end your presentation on a negative note —

even if your customer doesn't commit. A positive environment keeps the relationship open.

**Rule Number Six: Have a passion to learn.** People who have a desire to increase their knowledge and want to develop their job skills are typically better closers because they are open to new information. They keep a pool of information available for their use.

This doesn't mean you should overwhelm your customer with product information, rather use your knowledge to more effectively relate how your product will satisfy your customer's needs.

**Rule Number Seven: Keep your momentum.** The best closers continually ask questions during their presentations. Questions prevent customers from stalling, whereas statements tend to force people into stalls.

**Rule Number Eight: Don't accept *no* for an answer.** A successful closer ends all transactions on a positive note. If a customer is not committing to purchase from you, at least close the transaction by repeating an affirmation you received from them regarding your product or service. Keep the door open.

## SELL EASY TIPS

- Closing is dependent upon the entire sales presentation.

- To receive a confirmation of a sale, you must have a base of affirmations.

♦ If you can't close a transaction, avoid shutting the door on future sales opportunities with the customer. Be positive.

# BUILD FUNCTIONAL RESPONSES

ALL OF US GREW UP SAYING CERTAIN THINGS IN CERTAIN ENVIRON-ments. For instance, when an adult said, "Eat everything on your . . ." you knew what was coming next, right? The same thing applies to sales. A customer isn't going to ask, "Who sets your prices?" Instead they will ask, "Why are your prices so high?"

The challenge for you is to learn how to respond to your customers' questions by building functional responses that come naturally and convincingly.

For example, a customer walks up to the meat counter in a grocery store. "Wow," he says. "Your meat prices are high." If the person behind the counter gets defensive and responds, "I don't set the meat prices. You'd better talk to the manager," the customer will not be satisfied.

If, however, the meat clerk had a functional response to use in this situation the customer would react more positively. The clerk could say, "Yes, our prices are a bit higher than others, but we only sell the freshest and most select cuts of meat. We guarantee your satisfaction. That is what our customers pay for - and get. What specific cuts of meat are you looking for?" This answer reassures the customer that the extra value justifies the higher price.

*A functional response expresses your confidence and trust in the value of your product. You will have greater success in sales by developing responses to typical customer questions and objections.*

In any business environment, whether you are selling to consumers, businesses, or industries, the challenge is to know what to say, when you need to say it, and in a manner that creates a connection between your customer and your product or service.

Additionally, you must respond confidently, so your customer can trust what you say. The words you use must come from your heart. You must believe them to be true.

Sell Easy Example:

I believe Fleetwood Coleman camping products and folding trailers are some of the finest products on the market. When I respond to questions about their tenting fabric, their seamless roofs, and all of the other features, I am repeating functional responses that I created - based upon my belief in Fleetwood's superiority.

Personal values are very important when you create functional responses to your customers' questions and hesitations. A functional response is something you determine to say in reply to a specific question or to handle a common resistance.

For example, when a customer says, "Why are your fees so high?" A functional response could be, "I appreciate you bringing that up. You see we customize our approach to our product. We single out your objectives to ensure you get the results you want. Our customers are willing to invest a little more of their dollars to get these kinds of results. Aren't you?"

When building functional responses, consider the following:

♦ In what situations do you need to respond to be successful?

♦ What do you need to say to validly support your product?

♦ In terms of the words you choose and the inflection of your voice, how can you best express your excitement in your product and your interest in your customer's needs?

## CREATING A FUNCTIONAL RESPONSE

The first step is to analyze the types of questions and resistance you most often get from your customers. More than likely you will find several common areas of concern.

The second step is to sit down and create a response to use in these re-occurring situations. Practice these responses until they become second nature to you. Your sincerity when responding to your customers is essential.

Following are some important elements to consider when you sit down to create functional responses to use in situations in which you often find yourself.

**Your functional responses should build value around your product or service.**
What do you want to say to your customers about the value or the uniqueness of your product? Is it the quality? Is it your ability to deliver the product to the customer when they need it? Is it your knowledge of their industry? Your response should emphasize the value of what you're selling.

**Responding to price is a typical challenge.**
Most customers are concerned with the costs of doing business. Therefore, at some point you will be challenged about the price of your product or service. You will need to build a functional response that links the value of your product or service to your price. Show how the benefits your customer will receive far outweigh any price difference between you and a competitor.

**Nurture momentum by using responses that make sense to your customers and that validate your product or service.**
When you share three or four benefits of your product — and you do it confidently — you create a momentum in your sales presentation that gets more yes. Help your customers make purchase decisions based on how you can satisfy their needs and wants. Then you will have greater success in making the sale.

### Respond to reluctance certainly.

Most customers are reluctant to make a buying decision. Usually their reluctance is based on the fact they need reassurance that what they are purchasing is really what they want. In this case, your functional response should verify their need and reinforce how your product or service satisfies it.

Sometimes customers haven't shopped around or compared you with other vendors. (See Chapter Five.) They want some validation before making a decision. Your functional response should alleviate your customers' concerns and help them make their purchase decision confidently.

### Respond to negative statements.

When a customer says something negative about your product, your service, or your business you should have a functional response ready. What if they've had a bad experience with you or your company? What are you prepared to say? Can you respond in a way to support the quality of your product? Can you assure your customer that what you bring to them is something that will meet their needs?

### Acknowledge a benefit.

Share with your customers the benefits they will receive by purchasing your product or service. Make it personal to them.

> Sell Easy Example:
>
> "You know, I can deliver the product on the date you requested. I have a number of customers who have the same time frame you do. I can assure you, through the guarantees we provide in our delivery system, that you will have the product when you need it."

This functional response is truthful and believable. It is an insurance factor for your customers. But again, it is a functional response. It is something you develop to say in a specific environment.

> **Caution:** *Sometimes customers make statements without wanting validation. They are just talking. For instance, when a customer says, "I have not been satisfied with this product before" they might not want a response from you. Rather than defend the quality of your product or service, find out what bad experience they had. In this environment your functional response would be a question.*

## SELL EASY RULES

**Rule Number One: Building functional responses will typically make your presentation more spontaneous.** When a customer asks a question or raises a common objection, you won't sit back and wait for a response to come to you, because you will have a functional response on the tip of your tongue. Your conversation will be more spontaneous and convincing. This is important. If you're not spontaneous with your responses you can create a de-motivated environment; and actually give your customer a reason to resist making a decision.

**Rule Number Two: Practice will improve your confidence.** The longer you work in business the more you will realize people raise similar objections. You will have the opportunity to practice your functional responses. And the more often you use your responses, the smoother and more confident you will sound, and the more effective your presentation will be.

**Rule Number Three: Ask questions to maintain momentum with your functional responses.** Your functional responses can alleviate concerns or doubts your customers may have.

> Sell Easy Example:
>
> When a customer tells you they "want to think it over" you can respond: "I appreciate that, Bob. Usually when someone says they want to think it over, it's not because they don't want to go ahead. Rather they want to make sure that when they go ahead with the purchase it is exactly what they thought it would be. Would you please share with me some of the things you still have questions about?"

Talk with your customer to analyze what they need to decide on before they move ahead. Typically what happens is your customer will bring up something new, like "You know, we need the product delivered by next Friday, but if we can get it on Thursday, that would be better. Is there any chance we could get it on Thursday?"

*Asking questions such as, "What needs to be resolved before you make a final decision?" or "At this point, what is keeping you from going ahead with a decision?" generates important information from your customers.*

This is indicative of the types of information you can acquire by effectively responding to your customers - and this information moves you ever closer to getting a yes.

**Rule Number Four: Put your functional responses on cards so you can practice them.** In school we learned our multiplication tables by practice, practice, and practice. The same principle holds true for building functional responses. If you want to say something to another person with conviction, you must practice saying the words. Years ago someone told me, "If you don't write it down, how can you ever improve it?"

I truly believe certain words or phrases evoke negative (or positive) reactions from people. If you don't take the time to analyze the words you use, you may never realize the reactions your words cause. Unfortunately, once you've said something, it's tough to go back and repair the damage, especially if you're not sure what word caused the reaction.

**Rule Number Five: Associate a number with a functional response.** Psychologists have determined that fragrances directly stimulate the brain. Without being processed, a fragrance can bring back memories and arouse a particular response. A fragrance is something in your mind that attaches to an experience.

Numbers are the same. In football, plays are numbered because a number immediately stimulates the players' brains about what is going to happen. Years ago, I began to assign numbers to the different functional responses I use. After associating each response with a specific number, my brain automatically responds to certain situations. For example, when someone says, "Your price is a little high" my brain pulls out number five. When someone says, "We really want to think it over" my brain pulls out number twelve. These responses are anchored in my mind.

## REVIEW

By following these tips you can build functional responses around the most common situations you encounter in business. When a customer brings up an issue that's important to them, you will know how to effectively respond to them — without having to sit back and say, "Well, where did that one come from?" or "I've heard that before."

## SELL EASY TIPS

- ◆ Develop specific positive responses to common situations.

- ◆ Become aware of situations that require a better response from you.

- ◆ Practice your functional responses so they come naturally and convincingly to you.

# Chapter Thirteen

# GIVE CHOICES

ONE OF THE RESPONSIBILITIES OF ANY SUCCESSFUL SALESPERSON IS to help customers sift through the myriad of products and services that are available in the market. Every salesperson wants their products and services to be in the forefront of their customers' minds. They want their customers to choose to do business with them.

That is the challenge. How do you guide your customers toward your product or service without confusing them?

According to Ray Kroc, founder of McDonald's, the key to having your customer choose you is to offer them choices — choices of your products and services. "Every customer needs choices, but," he warned, "don't confuse a customer with too many choices." Ray's rule was to offer customers three choices, and never more than four.

What kinds of choices do you give your customers? My guess is most salespeople don't do a very good job offering their customers a choice. Recently a client was telling me about how he gave one of his customers a great choice. I asked, "How many choices did you give them?"

He responded, "Well, one. They told me what they wanted and I told them what I could do."

"Then you've probably forced your customer into shopping you against somebody else," I said, "because you only gave them one choice of how you could solve their problem."

When you give your customer one choice, you're saying, "That's it." It's something or nothing. When a financial planner says to a customer, "Joe, I want to help you secure your retirement. This is our product," they are challenging Joe to shop them against somebody else, because they've only given Joe one choice. Instead, the financial planner should say, "Joe, there are three primary packages I can offer you based on your unique needs."

## PACKAGING

The key to offering choice is to package effectively. Choices can be determined by packaging color, model, features, delivery, payment, follow up service, etc.

> Sell Easy Example:
>
> A customer is interested in a manufactured home. The packages (choices) he is offered are:
>
> **Package A:** the house delivered to a building site and laid onto the foundation. Cost: $50,000.
>
> **Package B:** the house delivered to a building site and

laid onto the foundation. The builder will also hook-up utilities, including septic and well. Cost: $65,000.

**Package C:** We help you select the right lot, the right placement and elevation for the home, then the house is delivered to the site you've selected. Also includes hook-up of utilities, septic and well. Cost: $75,000.

In the retail arena, accessories are essential to packaging. Let's return to the lawn mower dealer. Although his shop is full of lawn mower accessories, he soon realizes that as stand alone items the accessories are not selling. He wants his customers to buy the accessories — but they don't. Why not? Because the choices are detached. They aren't connected to the mowers. Remember that most customers want to make one purchase decision. The more decisions a customer has to make, the more complicating it is for the customer. They will hesitate to make multiple decisions at one time.

*Give your customer choices of you, you and you — not you and someone else.*

The dealer gets smart and decides to offer a basic riding mower for $1,500. That's his **benchmark product.** It is the lowest price he will offer his customers. Then he adds accessories to the benchmark product. He adds a double bag recycler and a mulcher to the riding mower, and offers this second choice for $2,000.

But, this still isn't enough choice. Ray Kroc said: "The minute you add a third choice for your customer you will sell easier and receive more loyalty than ever before." It is the third choice that is magic with a customer because you go from selection to choice. Selection is two. Choice is three. The third choice has to be extended in terms of value, but not extended in terms of price.

So, the dealer adds a snow blower to the riding mower with the double bag recycler. He knows this is what his customers really need and want. He puts a price of $2,300 on this third package.

In essence, what the dealer has done is taken a $1,500 benchmark product and marketed it against a $2,000 and a $2,300 choice. By offering his customers three choices, he not only holds their interest in his products; he will also sell more of the $2,300 packages — because there is only a $300 difference "for that extra product." He has added a greater perceived value.

If you ask his customers why they chose the $2,300 package, more than likely their response would be: "It's only $300 more — and look — I get everything I want."

The same philosophy of choice is valid in any business. If you put a primary choice here and an accessory choice on the wall, your customer will think that by buying an accessory they're increasing their cost. They won't take the accessory off the wall.

Don't put the accessories on the wall and the product on the floor. It's another decision for your customer. And the more decisions, the more complicated it is for your customer.

This packaging concept is very evident in the automotive industry. When dealers sell new cars, customers have a choice of accessory packages, rather than having to decide on numerous individual features and add-ons. Three choices are much easier for the customer.

## SELL EASY RULES

**Rule Number One: Offer at least three — but never more than four — choices.** How can you take your product or your service and accessorize it into three choices for a customer? Each of the choices would cost the customer a little bit more, but each choice would be more valuable to your customer. And the more value a product offers, the less perception there is of a greater cost.

**Rule Number Two: Build vertical packages.** How can the same product be worth more based upon what features and benefits you add to it? Notice what the dealer did with the riding lawn mowers. You should do the same with your product and service. Rather than give your customer a choice of accessories, give them a choice of vertical packages.

There are several benefits you can add to vertically position almost any type of product or service. The challenge today is that too many businesses provide premium services — without charging their customers for the service, when, in fact, the service is valuable. The result is that customers are beginning to perceive service, in and of itself, to be a free commodity, instead of something they should pay for.

> Sell Easy Example:
> If your customer wants to buy 100 units from your company, ask them, "Do you want it shipped tomorrow via next day air or is ground service what you prefer?" That's an accessory choice. The sooner they want to receive the package, the more value the add-on is — cand the more you can charge for it.

**Rule Number Three: Price vertically.** You want to offer your customers three different levels of pricing. You should

SELL EASY!

always spread the difference in price between package A and B wider than you split the price difference between package B and C. Make your greatest value choice the smaller margin difference. (Refer to the manufactured home example on page 124.) This strategy creates upward mobility by giving your customer the deal on the higher end of the scale.

The difficulty many companies face is they offer their customers three choices, but they don't have them priced correctly. They wonder why more customers aren't buying the most expensive choice. Inevitably it is because the margin between the middle package and the high-end package are too far apart.

**Rule Number Four: Build a price spread that adds value to the top.** Your benchmark product probably won't sell, because it will be compared to similar basic models offered by other vendors. But you can grab your customers' attention by offering them at least two more choices — both of which have more value for the price difference. If you ask a customer why they chose the $2,300 mower the most likely response will be: "because it was only $300 more." Of course, in essence it was $800 more, because you benchmarked your primary product.

**Rule Number Five: Make the lowest choice your average choice.** To encourage your customers to move up in their purchase habits your goal should be to give two choices *above* what the average customer buys from you. This concept relates to the scenario of small, medium and large soft drinks. Someone at McDonald's finally questioned, "Why are we offering small? We'll offer regular, medium and large sizes." What happened is that the medium became the regular. Everything was upgraded, and the customer's average spending increased — without complaint on the part of the customer — cbecause they believed they were getting more (value) for their money.

Don't offer a package *below* your average price. Companies that offer their customers a choice below and a choice above their average will have difficulty in stimulating upward movement in their average sales. You must give two choices above your average to get upward momentum.

## REVIEW

By offering your customers choices you will improve the relationship you have with them because your customers will become excited about being able to choose between you, you, and you.

## SELL EASY TIPS

♦ Understand the importance of giving your customers three valid choices based on your product or service.

♦ A selection of quantity does not constitute offering your customer a choice. Choices must be based on benefits and satisfying your customer's needs.

♦ Offer a selection of choices that add value to the highest product or service. To do this, keep the margin between your middle and high-end product less than the margin between the low-end and the middle product.

## Chapter Fourteen

# OVERCOME RESISTANCE

RESISTANCE FROM CUSTOMERS IS PART OF THE BUYING PROCESS. IT is a natural step people go through before they are ready to say, "Yes, I want to take advantage of your service" or "Yes, I think this product would be great for me."

If you find yourself at the point of asking a customer to make a final decision, and you haven't encountered any resistance, they probably aren't serious about making a purchase decision. Or you haven't been effective in bringing them to the point of saying yes.

Let me explain. If you don't encounter resistance or your customer hasn't questioned their final decision, then maybe your customer doesn't realize you're asking them for a final yes. You want to be sure your customer is positive about your product or service and that you've put them in an environment where it's easy for them to say yes. You want to avoid asking a customer to make a decision that they either don't want to make or that they aren't prepared to make.

If someone is excited about what you sell and they view the purchase as an opportunity that will benefit them and/or their company, then any resistance you encounter can be overcome by using the strategies in this chapter.

I want to emphasize again though, that your goal is to match the value of your product or service to the highest level of your customer's need, and then to make it easy for them to give you a yes. This is where resistance comes into play. In order to reach the point of a yes, most customers will naturally demonstrate some resistance.

## URGENCY

There are three levels of urgency for a customer. The level that they are at will determine how much time and effort you will need to put forth to close the sale. It will also determine what type of information you need to give your customer to have them feel comfortable saying yes.

A **level one** customer has a why and a when. They have a reason to take advantage of your product or service, and they have a buying cycle or a time line in mind. Usually these are the easiest customers to work with because you don't have to establish a time line. When you ask them, "When were you planning on making a decision about purchasing this?" and they say, "We'd like to get this taken care of by next Thursday" they've told you they're a level one customer.

Anyone with a need for your product or service and is in

the buying cycle will exhibit less resistance to the purchasing process.

A **level two** customer has a why but no when. They have a reason to take advantage of your product or service, but the pressure to make a purchase is not great enough for them to have established a time line. From a strategic standpoint, you help a level two customer by asking them when questions. This strategy can be applied to any product or service you sell:

♦ "When were you planning on making a decision about this?"

♦ "How soon would you like to begin our service?"

♦ "How quickly would you like to have your employees in our training program, so they can better understand your company's goals?"

♦ "When would you like your investment to return these kinds of dollars for your financial security?"

You should be most concerned about level three customers. These customers have no why or when — although they act interested. All salespeople, regardless if you're in traditional or nontraditional sales, deal with these customers every day.

**Level three** customers hang onto every word you tell them. They are interested in everything you say to them — but they don't have a reason to buy your product and there is no urgency to make a purchase.

Maybe they don't have the job responsibility of a buyer. They are not the decision-makers. Instead their task is to collect data and information so that someday someone else can make a decision. They only compile files of information on your product or service.

Or they are shoppers. They spend time gathering interesting information with which they will do absolutely nothing.

Sell Easy Example:

A friend of mine who manages a major travel agency says that about sixty of the people who telephone the agency on any given day are the same people who call every month, planning a trip to a place they will never visit. They call to check out airfares and accommodation prices regularly — with no intent on actually travelling.

Can you imagine how much time and energy a level three customer can take out of your workday? If they are not quantified or qualified level three customers could conceivably expend your business resources. I'm not saying you need to be tough on these people, but I do think it's important to allocate your time wisely based on which level the customer is at.

As a matter of fact, many traditional salespeople spend more time with level three customers than they do with level ones or level twos — because level three customers do not give them any resistance. Level three customers are truly accepting to everything you say. The resistance phase of the selling cycle never comes up. Too many salespeople fall into the trap of thinking this is the greatest thing about their jobs — customers who don't say no.

Unfortunately, time spent on level three customers, however enjoyable, is usually fruitless.

Resistance is a part of making a sale. Even a level one customer will give you some resistance. With a level two customer you can bring them to the point of resistance by asking "when" questions.

## STALLS

The challenge you have in dealing with resistance are the stalls. Stalls occur when a customer sit back and lets the pressure build so high that they can't make a final decision. Stalls can happen for any number of reasons.

Sometimes stalls occur because you have truly met with a level of resistance. Resistance comes in two forms. It can be an **objection** or it can be a **condition.**

An **objection** is when your customer raises a concern that might not be valid in terms of moving ahead with the purchase, but they use it as a way to stall the transaction. For example, they might have the money budgeted, but they tell you your price is too high. You need to determine if this is an objection or a condition. An objection is when the price is a little high — but the customer has the money in their budget.

A **condition** is an impediment to the sale. A condition is when a customer doesn't have the money in their budget to cover the expense. If a customer raises a condition when a salesperson is trying to close the sale it is an indication they did not effectively quantify or qualify the customer in advance. Most conditions that occur when you're trying to get the yes, tend to be the result of a failure to effectively ask questions earlier in the sales presentation.

> Sell Easy Example:
>
> You reach the point of asking your customer to make a purchase decision and the customer says they are not the one who will make the final decision. If this is the

first time you were aware your customer was not the decision-maker — it is your fault, not theirs. You have placed the customer in a condition environment by failing to ask the right questions, like, "Who else needs this information before a final decision is made?"

Stalls also occur when a salesperson lacks information. For instance, a customer says, "We will consider going ahead with the purchase. How soon can you install it?" If the salesperson can't answer the question without first checking other sources, he may cause a stall. An alternative to a stall in this situation is to anchor the customer's agreement based on the outcome of the research.

Sell Easy Example:

**Customer:** "Can we get this done by Friday?"

**Sell Easy Person:** "If we can supply this by Friday, it's a go, right?"

Anchor the agreement based upon the answer to their question. Validate the fact that they will go ahead with the purchase based on your positive response to their question. Then you can go to a final agreement without having to re-verify — and that's critical in the sales process.

## STRATEGIES

There are two strategies you can use to handle a stall or reluctance on the part of your customer. One is moving to an open-probed question. (See Chapter 8.) When a customer says, "We aren't planning on doing anything right now" or "You know, we're planning on waiting until the third quarter of the year" you must be prepared to ask an open-probed question to avoid a stall. Common stalls are:

- Price
- Happy with current vendor/status quo
- "I'm not the decision maker"
- We just started looking

By asking an open-probed question you can ignore the little voice inside of your head that says, "Well, here it is again. They're not going to move ahead with a purchase." To prevent stalls in the conversation ask, "When in the third quarter are you planning on making your decision?" or "What have we already discussed that you would like to reaffirm before you make your decision in the third quarter?" By asking these questions you bring the future into today.

Sell Easy Example:

**Customer:** "We don't have the budget for this item now, but we will have it budgeted in our next fiscal year. So, we will probably make a decision in the new year."

**Sell Easy Person:** "What are you planning on budgeting in the new year to facilitate your investment in this product?"

Sometimes customers ask hard fact questions. By asking open-probed questions in return, you can avoid a stall.

Sample hard fact questions are:

- "Can we get 2,000 widgets by Monday?"
- "Can the system be operational by next month?"
- "Can I buy in the stock market by next week's opening?"

Open-probed questions to avoid a stall:

- If I can deliver 2,000 by Monday, you'll place the order?

- If the system is installed and operational by next month, you'll move ahead with the purchase?

- If I can assure your activity in next week's opening of the stock market, you'll sign with me?

The second strategy that is effective in dealing with customer resistance is called the **four-step approach**. First you soften the response. Then you rephrase what the customer says so you can respond to it in step number three, which is to answer and deal with it so you can move into verification, which is step number four.

**Step one is a softening response.** Assure your customers it is okay for them to say what they did. Let them know they are not wrong to resist, because ultimately this is the level of communication you want with your customers.

> Sell Easy Example:
>
> A customer resists. "Gee, the price of your product is higher than what we expected." You reply, "I appreciate that. I've talked with other people who felt the same way before they went ahead. When they analyzed the cost benefit of our product it helped them understand why we were their best choice. Let's review the numbers again."

**Step two is to rephrase what they said so you can relate to the statement.**

> Sell Easy Example:
>
> **Customer:** "The price of your product is a little high."
>
> **Sell Easy Person:** "Many people said the same thing until they looked at the cost-value benefit of our product. I think, Mike, it's not necessarily the additional cost but the long-term benefit of a valuable relationship that

is important to you, right? We ensure that after installation you won't have extra costs popping up. And, we'll be here to give you service."

Always tie down your rephrase to get an agreement. If you say, "The cost over time is more important to you than price, isn't it?" and they answer no, then you have to go back to the issue of price. You need to talk about how much money they have budgeted, and resolve any other concerns they might have.

The positive aspect to this resistance is that it gives you the opportunity to validate that your customer does agree with you — before you get to a closing environment.

**Step three is to answer their question.**

Sell Easy Example:

You could do a cost analysis that shows over the next six years how this is a zero-cost investment for your customer. Explain that by installing a total comfort system with an efficiency level of 92 percent, in a six-year time frame, it costs them nothing to install the total comfort heating/cooling system. Over six years the savings in utility bills offsets the entire $7,000 of retrofitting their system today. Ask your customer, "Are you planning on staying in this building for the next six years? You must resolve the issue of price before moving on."

**Step four is to verify their final agreement. Once you've answered their question, you need to re-verify their agreement.**

Sell Easy Examples:

"Mike, based upon cost analysis, do you agree that as long as you plan on using the system for six years it's a zero-cost item?" Verify he agree it's a wise investment.

~

**Customer:** "We would like to think this over. I think this is a great opportunity."

**Sell Easy Person:** "I understand this is a major decision. Anyone making a decision like this, with the amount of dollars that you're going to invest, wants to be sure they've got all the facts right before deciding. I suspect what you're telling me (step number two) is it's not that you're not planning on going ahead, rather you want to make sure all the points are covered before you make a final decision, right?"

**Customer:** "Yes."

**Sell Easy Person:** "Then let's cover the critical factors to make sure your decision is correct." *Then you go through them. (Usually I review four. Any more than four tends to get complicated.)* Based upon a response to the four facts, "Is there anything at this point that's standing in your way of making a final decision?" If there is, respond accordingly.

## SELL EASY RULES

**Rule Number One: Resistance is a natural part of the selling process.** If you haven't met with any resistance, you need to determine why. Either your customer is not the decision-maker or your presentation hasn't been effective in bringing your customer to the point of saying yes. Ultimately, you need to ask questions to determine why you're not meeting with resistance.

**Rule Number Two: Before making a final purchase decision a customer needs a sense of urgency — both a why and when.** Without a need (why) and a time line to satisfy the need (when) your customer may not resist any part of your presentation. Be wary of customers who agree with everything you say. It is too good to be true! You might be spending time on a level three customer — someone who has no plans to actually make a purchase.

**Rule Number Three: An objection to a purchase can be overcome, whereas a condition is a very real impediment to the sale.** By asking questions, you can discover which situation you have.

> Sell Easy Example:
>
> A realtor shows a home to two couples. Couple A objects to the listed price. Couple B objects to the listed price. By pre-qualifying (asking questions) the realtor will be able to determine if they are merely objecting to the price (trying to bargain) or if the house is simply out of their price range. Once the realtor has this information, he can spend his time accordingly.

## Review

Once you acknowledge and accept that resistance is a necessary element of the sales process — and you begin to look forward to the opportunity to overcome your customers' resistance — you will get more yes.

## Sell Easy Tips

- Realize that resistance is a normal part of the buying process.

- Handle resistance by acknowledging your customer's position and by asking questions.

♦ Understand the difference between a stall and an impediment to the sale.

♦ Be confident in your ability to move customers out of a stall.

Chapter Fifteen

# How to Handle
# Price Objections

CUSTOMERS ARE SENSITIVE TO PRICE. RESEARCH SHOWS THAT ON average twenty-seven percent of your customers getting the best price is their main objective, while fifty-six percent of your customers can't decide if they should base their purchase decision on price or value. That leaves only seventeen percent who realize the value in your product or service.

These statistics reinforce the need for salespeople to learn how to effectively sell products and services based on value — not price. This is quite a challenge in today's market, since customers often talk with your competitors, who tell your customers that they offer the same product — at a lower price. To keep your customers' interest and business, you must know how to address this situation.

As you prepare your presentation on handling price objections, remember :

### Price minus cost equals value.

To respond effectively to a price objection you must first understand that *price* is the money your customer pays up front. *Cost* is related to keeping the product over time — the value of the service over time. Does it need to be repair-ed or maintained? Will it wear out? Does the response time for service exceed the customer's level of need? How will my business benefit from this service or training? Are there ongoing benefits as a result of this service?

If a customer buys a product but can't get it repaired, the cost factor increases dramatically. If the product wears out faster than expected — the cost goes up. Even though the customer may have paid a lesser *price* for the product, quality and durability affect the actual *cost*.

> Sell Easy Example:
>
> If a dealer sells a car that requires less maintenance than a competitor's car, his car actually costs less — even if the price of the car is $1,000 more than the competitor's model. The fact a customer doesn't have to hassle with maintenance as often, or experience the frustration of dealing with uncooperative service people offsets the price. The $1,000 difference in price is diminished by the cost of having the car serviced more frequently.

Price minus cost equals the true value over time. After a short period of time, the cost is well worth the thousand-dollar difference in terms of service, response, and durability.

Your challenge, then, is to effectively define the difference between price and cost for your customer. If you charge a higher price but your product lasts significantly longer than the competition's, what happens to the cost? The cost goes down and the value goes up. Once you show the value of your product or service, in terms of your customer's needs, their objection to price is effectively answered.

This is the concept that is behind most name-brand loyalty. Over time consumers come to expect a certain value from specific name-brand products. Although consumers may not be able to verbalize why they are committed to a specific brand — the fact is they believe it is a valuable product. The product they rely on may not be the least expensive, in terms of actual price, but it is in terms of cost to them. Consumers will pay more for value — because they know that in the long run, the cost is actually less.

Customers will base the cost of making a purchase on the following ten elements. Your goal should be to incorporate these elements into your sales presentations, so that you effectively respond to any price objections you receive.

**1. Ease of making the purchase.**
If you want customers to buy your product you must make your product available to them and easy to purchase. A good example of this concept in a retail environment is Target department stores. Target's management realizes that customers like to ask questions, so Target places customer service personnel in all of the store's departments. By doing this, customers find shopping at Target easier. They know if they have a question or need help getting a product off the shelf, there will be a customer service rep nearby to assist them.

This extra attention to the customers' needs decreases the cost of shopping at Target while increasing the value of their products.

## 2. Reliability.

Customers relate reliability with cost. Will the product last a long time? Is it durable? Is the product easy to assemble? If the customer needs help assembling it — or understanding it (computer software, for example) can they get assistance over the phone easily?

## 3. Predictability.

Almost everything that relates to cost is a promise. The more tangible the promise, the more definable the value. If you tell your customer, "It's easy to bring this in for service," you've not given the customer anything tangible. It could be an empty promise. Instead, give an example of a customer who brought an item in for service and discuss the prompt and friendly service they received. Or, share a letter from a satisfied customer. Take your promise and make it tangible. Let your customer know what they can expect from you after the sale.

## 4. Satisfy their needs.

Customers will purchase a product if it will satisfy their needs. Usually a customer has multiple needs. The more needs you can satisfy, the less likely it is that the customer will object to price.

Sell Easy Example:

A successful computer salesman will sell more than hardware to satisfy her customers. She will discuss the help her customers will receive from the technicians to set-up the hardware and install the software. She will state that trained customer service reps are available by phone to assist with any questions the customer may have after the installation is complete. She will promise that she will follow up in a week to make sure the customer is happy with their purchase.

All of these extras will not only satisfy her customer's needs, they will also lower the cost and raise the value of the product.

**5. Customers want to save money, but not all customers demand the lowest price.**
Some customers realize saving isn't always related to price. Saving can be reflected in an easier transaction — or more personal service. It can be the difference between purchasing an airline ticket over the Internet versus visiting a local travel agency. The price offered on the Internet might be less — but the risk of dealing with a machine may not be worth it. Feelings are valuable. There may be more comfort in dealing with a person than with a machine. The cost of using the Internet may be too high if there is a problem with the transaction. What if a ticket for the wrong date or destination is issued? A lesser price is sometimes not considered a value.

**6. Knowledge. Competence. Follow-up.**
Customers appreciate the extra things you offer them. What knowledge do you have that makes you special? Does this knowledge help your customers? Do you exhibit competence and confidence in your sales presentations? Sending a card of appreciation to your customers immediately after a sale (not weeks later) is noticed — because it rarely happens. Even this post-sale gesture has the power to increase the value of the products you sell to your customers.

## 7. Total product offering.

Many times customers have specific needs. They may feel their circumstances are unique, and therefore they will seek a source that is specialized. One example would be a couple who is interested in a whole-house music system. Instead of visiting a variety of stores trying to piece the system together themselves, the homeowners will select a business that specializes in custom sound systems. A reliable custom sound system business will offer the homeowners the entire product: consultation, custom design, installation, and service. In other words, they offer the total product.

This is similar in a retail environment. When a customer wants the best of some product — whether they are in need of jewelry, a kite, or eyeglasses — they will visit a specialty store. Specialty stores don't have to stock a variety of different products — but they do have to offer the best selection of jewelry, kites, or eyeglasses.

## 8. Product knowledge.

Customers seek information about products and services. The key is to share valuable information about your product without overdosing your customer with data. Share the information your customer needs to know, the information that relates to their specific wants — so that they find it valuable — and not boring or overbearing.

## 9. Application knowledge.

Customers want to talk with someone who can apply the product to their environment — not just talk about the product. Discuss your product as it relates to your customer's business. Application knowledge increases your value.

## 10. Response.

What your customer receives after the sale is important. Reliability and predictability can significantly affect the quality of the product. Your response and the product's response must be tangible.

To handle price objections effectively, there are three critical things you should understand:

First, to offset the price of your product you must offer your customer the value of your knowledge.

To be valuable to your customers you should have product and need knowledge. You should be able to explain how your product relates to your customers' specific needs. You should know how your product can be used to achieve optimum results — which is application knowledge. Learn about your customers' industries so you can share industry information with them. Know and understand the environment in which your product or service is used.

> Sell Easy Example:
>
> A bank provides many services, including different types of checking accounts. The bank realizes that a customer's environment affects their needs. They know that a young couple with children has significantly different needs compared to a retired couple. These customers will write checks for different reasons. They will keep different amounts of money in their accounts. The checking accounts will be used for different purposes. The young couple is probably stretching their money and will be interested in overdraft protection, whereas the older couple may not access their account very often.

Environment matters. Environment dictates how you build value with each of your customers.

Second, even though your customer is objecting to your price, there is a reason that they are talking with you.

If your customer believed your price was too high, and they were truly not interested in your product or service, they wouldn't make the effort to talk with you, right? I believe the fact that a customer is sitting there and saying, "I really want to buy, but I can't deal with the price" is their way of saying, "I'm interested." They are trying to negotiate the price because they realize the value of your product or service. Take this distinction into account. They haven't said, "Your price is too high. Good-bye."

Third, no one sells exactly the same product or service — not even your closest competitor.

The challenge for you when handling price objections is to be able to support your difference by relating to the highest needs of your customer. You need to state your uniqueness (see Chapter 2) to offset the price objection. Your uniqueness could be your follow-up, your reliability, the quality of your product, or the personnel who will work with your customer after the sale. Find your uniqueness and highlight it for each customer.

## SELL EASY RULES

**Rule Number One: Your customer must be the buyer.** When you talk with a customer who is resisting price, make sure they have the responsibility to make the purchase decision. Sometimes the customer you are talking with doesn't have the authority to purchase; they are just looking. Maybe they've been sent out as scouts, to research your product. In my consulting business, there are people who contact me every year to review my services — but they have no intention of buying anything — they are just accessing my information and knowledge.

**Rule Number Two: Sell function, not form.** When you are trying to offset your price by establishing the value of your product, what your product does is more important than what your product is. What will your product do for your customer? The fact that a riding lawn mower will beautify your customer's yard is usually more important than the fact it has a twelve-horse power engine. It's the difference between function and form.

> Sell Easy Example:
>
> When my car dealer offers to service my car overnight, and pick up and return the car to me before I need it the following morning, I don't mind that the cost of an oil change may be double what I'd pay elsewhere. What the service is — an oil change — is of less importance to me than what it does — allows me to stay home while my car is serviced. And, most importantly, I don't mind paying extra for the oil because the biggest cost to me, not necessarily in terms of dollars but in terms of time, is getting my car to a service center for an oil change. The function of the service provided by my dealer has eliminated my objection to price.

**Rule Number Three: Sell the differences, not the similarities.** When a customer objects to the price of your product or service, don't try to rationalize your price by listing ten features of your product or service. Instead, discuss two or three unique benefits your product offers that your competition's doesn't.

**Rule Number Four: Define what quality means to your customer.** Ask your customer what three benefits of your product or service are most important to them. What do they expect as a result of making the purchase? Then review how your product will provide those benefits. Instead of stating, "This is what makes our product a quality item," explain how your product provides what they expect.

> *What your product does is more important than what your product is.*

**Rule Number Five: Demonstrate, don't present.** Encourage your customers to imagine using the product. Involve your customers in ownership. An example of this is a builder who walks a couple through a spec home. As they pass through the living room or den, he inquires where they would place their furniture. Instead of just walking them through the house and saying, "This is the living room. This is the den. Nice kitchen, huh?" He is giving them psychological possession.

**Rule Number Six: Sell to your customer's highest need.** I've said this before — but this crucial in handling price objections. Sell to the highest need of your customer. Your product could have the most advanced features, but if it doesn't satisfy your customer's greatest need, you'll never be able to overcome their objection to your price. If the product won't benefit them, the price will always be too high.

## SELL EASY TIPS

♦ Understand that price is the money your customer

pays up front. Cost is related to keeping a product over time — or the value of a service over time.

♦ You must define the difference between your selling price and the actual cost to your customers.

♦ To overcome price objections, satisfy your customers' greatest needs and wants.

# Chapter Sixteen

# RESPOND TO CUSTOMER INDECISION

WE'VE DISCUSSED TWO KEY FACTORS IN MAKING A QUALITY SALES presentation: understanding your customer's highest need and demonstrating how your product and service satisfies that need. To successfully close your transaction there is another critical task: knowing how to handle your customer's resistance.

The abundance of similar products and services on the market today makes it difficult for customers to make final purchase decisions. More than ever before, customers are insecure about making the right choice. An effective salesperson, therefore, must be skilled at handling the inevitable indecision - especially at the time of closing.

Typically when you are ready to ask your customer for that final yes — is when your customer feels at the greatest level of risk. Their common reaction to this feeling of risk or uncertainty is to hedge by coming up with stalls. When you are prepared for this indecision and anticipate the stall you will be able to lessen the risk, especially at this final stage of your presentation.

First, you need to define your customer's resistance as either indecision or a condition. Indecision is a reluctance to go ahead with the purchase. It is a stall. A condition is an impediment to the sale. (See Chapter 14) In this sell easy chapter we will discuss the philosophy of handling indecision.

The following five sell easy steps will guide you on how to respond effectively to your customers, and thereby reinforce their confidence in your product or service — and give them the support they need to say yes.

---

### Five common put-offs:

1. "It's too high priced."
2. "We weren't planning on making a decision today."
3. "I want to take a look around."
4. "Someone else is involved in the decision."
5. "This isn't quite what we're looking for."

---

**Step One: Acknowledge that you understand your customer's reluctance.**

Assure your customers that by voicing their concerns they have not jeopardized the transaction. For example, if your customer says, "Your price is too high" or "We're going to compare you with someone else" let them know it is okay. If you resist or argue with your customer, they may become more defensive and feel at a higher level of risk. When they become defensive customers are more inclined to say "no" rather than "let's talk about it." Show your customers you understand their positions.

**Step Two: Isolate the objection as your customer's only impediment to saying yes.**

The purpose of isolating the objection is to get your customer to agree to the value of your product or service. You want to confirm that once you handle the objection to their satisfaction they will agree to the sale.

---

### How to Respond to Common Put-offs:

1. Highlight the benefits of your product or service that relate to your customer's most important need.

2. Establish urgency. Ask your customer how important this product or service will be to their situation.

3. Remind the customer of your uniqueness.

4. Review your customer's needs to determine if your product or service does indeed satisfy them.

---

Sell Easy Example:

When a customer objects to the price you've quoted them, make sure that if it wasn't for the higher price, they would absolutely go ahead with the purchase.

**Customer:** "Your price is too high."

**Sell Easy Person:** "I appreciate you sharing that with me. Do you like the product (or service) I'm offering? Do you see the benefits it provides you? Do you see our uniqueness? Okay, let's focus on the difference in price then. Based upon what we've discussed, we're talking about $500 for our product versus $400 from Company X. Let's look at this $100 difference."

Then state three things that are very important to your customer that offset the $100. (This is where the data you've acquired by asking the right questions (Chapter 8) and your customer profiles (Chapter 3) help you target your presentation.) In this way, you can offset the $100 difference quickly and easily — and get ever closer to the final yes.

## Step Three: Rephrase your customer's objection.

To show that you understand the reason for your customer's indecision, paraphrase their objection. Usually I lead with "In other words, what you're telling me is...." or "If I'm hearing you clearly...".

Sell Easy Example:

**Customer:** "You know, I just started to look. I'm not planning on making any decisions today."

**Sell Easy Person:** "I understand where you're coming from. This is a major decision based upon your company's budget restrictions. You want to be sure you make the right choice, and that you get the right information. From what you've said, I sense that you believe in what we can deliver. You believe our product can benefit your company. Before you can decide, however, you want to be sure that the cost factor after the sale is what you expect. Is that correct?"

## Step Four: Discuss the benefits your customer will experience after the sale.

By discussing the benefits your customer will receive after the purchase you can alleviate most put-offs and indecision. Ask your customer to state what benefits they anticipate to receive by using the product or service. If your customer is unable to state any benefits, you must identify the benefits for them, based upon their needs. For example, in a business to business sale:

♦ Lower production costs.

♦ Improve employee job satisfaction.

♦ Streamline manufacturing processes.

♦ Expedite customer service.

## Step Five: Close the transaction.

Ask for the final decision by marrying your close to their final yes. For example, "Based upon what this compressor will do for you, and if I guarantee a service cost reduction, you will go ahead?"

## REMINDER

Always ask for agreements along the way to your close. The little yeses provide the foundation for a final agreement. When you isolate, you want agreement. When you rephrase, you want agreement. Understand. Isolate. Rephrase. Answer. And get the final yes.

To become skilled at handling indecision and put-offs, take time now to determine the top five put-offs you hear most often from your customers. Then review the five steps and design your personal response for each of these common put-offs.

## SELL EASY RULES

**Rule Number One: Identify the cause for the put-off.** Often it is important for you to determine why your customer is reluctant to make a final decision. If your customer says, "We weren't planning on going ahead right now," you should ask, "What two or three things do you have questions about before you decide?" Their answer will provide you with the information you need to respond effectively.

Sometimes your failure to make a thorough and effective presentation/demonstration is the cause for a stall. You probably haven't provided your customer with all of the information they need to answer their primary questions if they say, "Well, you're the first one we've looked at. Before we make a final decision we want to look at someone else." Had you made a no-name comparison earlier in your presentation (Chapter 2) you most likely would have avoided this situation.

**Rule Number Two: Reduce the level of risk.** There are two ways to reduce the level of risk or fear. The first is to move your customer into the benefits of usage by having them take psychological possession. A good example of this philosophy is letting a customer test drive a car or ride a bike. By doing this, your customer moves beyond the final decision into experiential usage. If your business doesn't allow for a hands-on experience, you can use pictures, collateral material, or verbally walk your customer through a particular scenario.

The second way to reduce the level of risk for your customer is to make a guarantee. Of course, you have to work within your own policy environment, but nonetheless, give your customer a guarantee of satisfaction. And — most importantly — sell the guarantee as a separate product. Don't treat the guarantee as a warranty or the warranty as a guarantee. Explain the uniqueness of your guarantee, because the guarantee is a feature of what you're selling.

**Rule Number Three: Ask benefit identification questions.** This is similar to taking your customer beyond the sale. A feature is what your product is, a benefit is what your product does specifically for your customer. To move your customer into benefit identification show how a particular feature of your product will satisfy their needs and wants.

Be careful not to overwhelm your customer. Recent studies show that consumers relate an over abundance of features with an increase in product price, while they relate an abundance of benefits with a reduction in actual cost.

The more features you identify that they don't need or want, the more your customer will feel pressured by price — because they anticipate they will be charged for each feature. However, the more benefits you identify, the less price pressure your customer feels — because they can identify with the benefits on a personal level of satisfaction.

Sell Easy Example:

A customer is buying a computer. The salesman discusses what the computer and accompanying software can do for the customer's marketing business. "Mr. Smith, what do you see as a benefit to this system?" The customer responds, "Wow! Do you realize how many clients I can profile, identify, search and target with this software?" The price ratio dropped significantly — because the customer was moved beyond the risk of making a purchase decision and into realizing the benefit of the product.

**Rule Number Four: Identify the urgency.** Always maintain an urgency to the purchase, especially if you encounter customer indecision. Ask about your customer's purchase time line up front. When does your customer want to start enjoying the benefits of the product or service? If there is no time line, create urgency by locking in a time and place for a follow-up visit to continue the transaction. Focus on how soon the customer would like to start benefiting from the product.

## REVIEW

Your goal should be to have responses available and ready when you hear a put-off. Practice response for the most common put-offs you receive. This preparation will help you attain more yes — throughout your business career.

## SELL EASY TIPS

- ◆ Define the five put-offs you receive most often and create responses that give you positive results.

- ◆ Determine if your customer's indecision is a stall or if it is an actual condition to the sale.

◆ By reinforcing your customer's confidence in your product or service you will be able to respond more effectively to their indecision.

◆ Practice, practice, and practice your responses to common customer indecision.

Chapter Seventeen

# GET MORE YES!

WHEN I ASK SALESPEOPLE WHAT THEY ENJOY LEAST ABOUT THEIR jobs, more often than not they tell me it's closing the transaction. In this sell easy chapter my goal is to show you how and why closing can be a comfortable part of your job. In reality, closing is nothing more than getting a final agreement, which is a natural conclusion to your well-structured presentation.

By the time you get to your closing, you've identified your customer's needs and wants - you've explained how your product or service satisfies those needs and wants - and you've received agreements from your customer. In other words, getting to the final yes is a logical culmination of the work you've already done.

Furthermore, once you acknowledge this fact, the pressure and apprehension you might feel at closing should disappear. Asking for the yes should be as pleasant as any other part of your presentation.

## STALLS DURING CLOSING

There are three approaches you can use if you hit a stall during your close:

**Sell Easy Approach One: Pre-agreements work well when you become stalled in the closing process.** "Of the three things we talked about, which would be your preference?"

**Sell Easy Approach Two: Re-state the positives.** Mention two or three things your customer agreed on earlier that you could build on. "Bob, I appreciate that at this time you might be reluctant to make a final decision. Let's review a couple of things, to make sure we're on the same wavelength." Then identify those two or three things.

**Sell Easy Approach Three: Another option is to reconfirm how your customer plans to buy, i.e. discuss the process of the purchase, not what they agreed to.** You might say something like, "Bob, you indicated you were going to set this up on a budgetary system (or you were planning on investing $400 each month)."

> Sell Easy Example:
>
> **Customer:** "We're not planning on going ahead right now. I'm not going to make a final decision now."
>
> **Sell Easy Person:** "Whether you make a final decision or not, Nancy, could I ask which of the three things we

talked about (identify three things — that's called item-
izing choices) would be your preference?"

**Customer:** "Well, it wouldn't be any of those three."

You now have what I call the builder process. You need
to discuss something they liked, whether it was one of
the choices or not, and build from there.

Let's say a customer comes to your shop wanting to purchase a riding lawn mower. You give him three choices. "We
have a 15-cubic inch with a 42-inch deck. We call that our
basic model. We have a deluxe model that is a little higher
priced — but it has a wind scoop on the front and a double
bag recycler on the back. Then we also have our ultra-deluxe
model, which not only has the wind scoop and the double
recycler, but it also has a CD player in the deck and comes
with our Gold Tag service contract."

Whether the customer decides to purchase the $1,500
tractor, the $2,000 tractor or the ultra-deluxe model for
$2,500, you have vertically merchandised three choices.
Your customer may not be inclined to buy any of these. But
by asking his preference of the three, you've removed the
pressure for a final yes - and you will gain insight about what
his purchase plans are.

## HOW TO ASK FOR A YES

There are three approaches you can use to get an agreement
to buy from your customer. Of course, anyone who has stud-
ied Closing 101 will argue there are over twenty ways to ask
a customer to make a decision. I have found, however, that
whatever type of sales you're in, the following three
approaches work best.

The first approach is to give your customer alternate choices. I call this the **alternate choice decision-making request**. The goal is to give your customer two or three choices, any one of which should generate a yes response.

If you're not as close to getting a final yes as you'd like to be, give your customer three choices. If, on the other hand, you feel you're close to a positive conclusion, give your customer only two alternate choices, rather than three. But, under no circumstances should you offer a customer more than three choices, because you will only confuse the situation.

The second approach to use is to **reach a minor conclusion related to a minor choice.** Break down the final agreement into two or three minor decisions. Get an agreement on the smaller steps that are a part of the overall decision.

> Sell Easy Example:
>
> "If you were going to purchase this product, Nancy, would it be this color?" or "Mike, if you went ahead, what would your monthly investment be, $400 a month?"

The third way to ask for an agreement is by **decisive action**. Decisive action is when you do something — your customer doesn't stop you — and their inaction indicates they are going ahead with the purchase.

**Examples of decisive action:**

♦ "I'll have the agreement ready for your signature on Tuesday. When on Tuesday would it be convenient for us to get together so you can sign it?" That says you're moving ahead. The action is you are going to put an agreement together for their approval.

♦ "Mike, we'll start your delivery on Thursday." That's decisive action, especially when you grab the phone to place the order.

♦ In a retail environment, putting a sold sign on a piece of artwork or a hold tag on a dining room set, is a physical action that is decisive.

♦ "I will assign someone to your account today. They will follow up with you on Tuesday to verify the final specs for delivery."

## SELL EASY RULES

**Rule Number One: Don't ask for a yes in a negative environment.** If you're dealing with an unhappy customer who is sharing information about things that aren't working well - and your customer is primed for a negative response - don't ask for the final yes. Instead re-verify things they have already agreed to.

For example, if a customer says, "I don't know whether I should go ahead" or "We've used this before and weren't happy," or "We've worked with people like you and been dissatisfied" return to something they were positive about.

Whenever you find yourself in a negative cycle during your closing presentation, re-verify a pre-determined yes, an anchor, and rebuild from that point forward. It's also beneficial to verify that your customer is still interested in making a buying decision.

**Rule Number Two: Get pre-agreement in the closing process.** Today, more than ever before, salespeople deal with customer indecision, stress, and lack of confidence. As a matter of fact, the market shows that some 56 percent of the people you ask to make a buying decision lack confidence in making that decision. Imagine. Fifty-six percent of your customers are confused when you're ready to close the transaction. This is why it is critical for you to initiate pre-agreement. Pre-agreement is nothing more than giving your customer choices and asking them for their preferences. (For all of you who have been in traditional sales, this is what we used to call "trial closing.) The idea is to have your customer explain where they stand in the decision-making process. And by giving them choices you remove pressure from the environment because you are merely asking them their preference - not for a final decision.

> Sell Easy Example:
> "Joe you could benefit from the $1,500 package, the $2,000 package, or the $2,500 package. If you were asked to choose now, which of these packages would you prefer? Why?"

Remember it's easier for a customer to make a final decision when they are presented with three choices. (See Chapter Thirteen.)

**Rule Number Three: Get advances if you can't close.** An advance is a question that keeps your customer in the decision-making mode. The purpose is to ask your customer to make a minor decision that can be applied to the final agreement. Advances are designed to move your customer forward toward a final decision.

There are many kinds of advance questions. They can be qualitative in nature. You can ask for your customer's opinion. You can schedule a follow-up appointment. They can be about someone else's involvement in the decision. The point is that they advance you toward the final decision. Sample advance questions are:

- "If you went ahead and placed the order, which of these colors would you prefer?"

- "Which day next week is most convenient for you to meet with me?

- "Who else do you want to share this information with before you make a final decision?"

*Get advances if you can't get conclusive agreement.*

**Rule Number Four: If you don't get a yes, confirm follow up.** If your customer does not give you a final yes, you need to follow up with them soon. You want to be sure your customer knows you consider the relationship active and the transaction still active.

Most important, the method and time of your follow up must be decided before you conclude the meeting with your customer. If you are going to make a follow-up phone call confirm a specific number and time. If you plan to meet in person confirm a location and time. You don't want to leave an environment where you've received some positive response — even if you haven't acquired a final yes — without confirming a follow-up meeting with your customer. Too much could be lost if you contact them later to schedule a follow-up meeting. You break the momentum of the relation-

---

## THREE WAYS TO ASK FOR AN AGREEMENT

**Number One:** alternate choice. Never give more than three choices to your customer. If you are at a point where you believe a yes is going to come sooner rather than later, offer two choices. If you think you're farther off and might get some resistance, offer three choices.

**Number Two:** minor conclusion. Break the decision down into minor points. Get the easy decisions first. Move into the tougher decisions as you go along.

**Number Three:** decisive action. Do something that indicates they've agreed to the purchase. If your customer doesn't object to your action, they are giving you a silent yes.

---

ship, which could destroy any positive results you've received thus far.

If you're in a traditional sales environment, you want to shorten the time between your last meeting and when you follow up. Statistics show that more than four or five days is too long to keep your customer waiting.

In a nontraditional environment (if your customer is inside your company), if you meet on Monday, you should follow up on Wednesday or Thursday to keep the decision-making cycle in motion. You don't want to start from ground zero again.

## OLD FAITHFUL

When your customer does not go ahead with an agreement you can always rely on an open-probed question to obtain information about their stall. This open-probed question is a single word: why. To personalize your question, be specific. "Why? Why at this point are you reluctant to make a decision?" or "Why at this point would you prefer to check with someone else?"

I've become very good at asking "Why?" Realize, though, you only ask this question of a customer who has indicated that what you're trying to sell is important to them. They have a need and a buying cycle.

You don't want to pressure someone who has not indicated they have a desire for your product or service. That kind of pressure is unfair to them...and certainly anyone else in the environment.

## SELL EASY TIPS

- ◆ Closing should be a comfortable part of your job — it's nothing more than the natural conclusion to a well-structured sales presentation.

- ◆ Avoid trying to close in a negative environment.

- ◆ Use the three approaches to get an agreement from your customer: alternate choice decision-making request, reach a minor conclusion, or by decisive action.

# Conclusion

Selling is easy, if you follow the techniques I've practiced over the years and outlined in this book. The key items to remember are:

1. Identify your category authority.

2. Develop a buying model of your best customers.

3. Manage your time well.

4. Discover the needs and wants of your customers by asking the right questions.

5. Sell the value (benefits) of your product or service as it relates to your customer's greatest needs.

6. Prepare and practice functional responses to common put-offs and customer indecision.

7. Give your customers three choices: you, you, and you.

8. Offset price objections by showing the difference between price and cost.

9. Realize reluctance is an inherent element of the buying cycle.

10. Relax. Closing is a natural conclusion to a well-structured sales presentation.

# INDEX

# ORDER INFORMATION

Obtain *Sell Easy* from your favorite bookstore.

If your bookstore does not have it in stock, you can order it directly for $24.95 plus $3.50 for shipping and handling per book. If five or more copies are ordered, send only $2.00 shipping and handling per book.

## Call 1-800-899-8971
**(credit card orders only)**

or

Please send _____ copies @ $24.95 _____

Shipping and handling at $3.50 per book _____
  ($2.00 per book for five or more copies)

**TOTAL:** _____

### PLEASE PRINT

Name_____

Address_____

City_____State_____ Zip_____

Phone (____)_____

Credit Card #_____Exp._____

Name on Card _____

Signature _____

Mail order blank with check or money order payable to
*St. Thomas Press* to:

**St. Thomas Press**
**3300 Edinborough Way, Suite 701**
**Minneapolis, MN 55435**

**www.winninger.com**

175